SENIOR ADULT MINISTRY
IN THE 21ST CENTURY

STEP-BY-STEP
STRATEGIES FOR
REACHING PEOPLE
OVER 50

DR. DAVID P. GALLAGHER

Wipf & Stock
PUBLISHERS
Eugene, Oregon

Wipf and Stock Publishers
199 W 8th Ave, Suite 3
Eugene, OR 97401

Senior Adult Ministry in the 21st Century
Step-By-Step Strategies for Reaching People Over 50
By Gallagher, Dr. David P.
Copyright©2002 by Gallagher, Dr. David P.
ISBN: 1-59752-663-0
Publication date 5/1/2006
Previously published by Group Publishing, 2002

CONTENTS

DEDICATION

This book is dedicated to Palm West Community Church in Sun City West, Arizona, a loving and faithful congregation that taught me important words in life: patience, faithfulness, sensitivity, balance, and (with sixteen retired pastors—at the time of this writing—within the congregation) biblical integrity. We have had an amazing journey together, and I love you deeply.

To my wife, Mary Ann, who has been my faithful partner, companion, friend, lover, and co-worker in ministry for the past thirty-four years. Her patience, dedication, loyalty, and faithfulness are an example to all.

To my two children, Rod and Kerri, who are gifts from God and who have amazingly achieved God's best and have survived and grown through some of life's toughest storms, not the least of which is that of being minister's kids!

To my parents, who are with the Lord and who taught me so much about life as a senior adult.

Finally, to Harold and Arvilla Garner, who were on the Christian education faculty at the Moody Bible Institute when I was a student there. They believed in me and shaped my biblical philosophy of Christian education and local church ministry.

INTRODUCTION

America's youthful face is changing! Consider these statistics:

- According to the 2000 U.S. Census, more than 76 million Americans (more than 25 percent of the population) are fifty or older.
- By 2040, when the last baby boomers reach retirement age, 25 percent of the American population will be over sixty-five.
- Life expectancy recently climbed to seventy-five years of age.
- In 1988, Modern Maturity Magazine became the nation's number one magazine in circulation, passing Reader's Digest, Time Magazine, and TV Guide.[1]
- "Two-thirds of all persons sixty-five or older who have *ever* lived are alive today! American seniors now outnumber the entire population of Canada."
- Since 1900, ten years have been added to the median age of the U.S. population.
- Since 1950, the number of Americans over one hundred years has grown more than ten times.
- By 2080, the number of senior adults who are over the age of one hundred is expected to increase by a factor of 75.[2]
- "In 1960, those 60 years old and over [of the world population] numbered 250 million (8.2 percent of the total population), and by 1980, the number had increased to 376 million (8.5 percent of the total). Projections indicate that those 60 and over will number 600 million (almost 10% of the total) by the year 2000 and over 950 million by 2020 (12.5 percent of the total)."[3]

We truly are seeing the aging of a nation. As a result, churches of all sizes are facing the needs of maturing adults. The challenge has reached both rural and inner city congregations among all ethnic groups. It impacts all denominations, all professions, and all states.

The conclusion? Pastors, church leaders, and lay people must be equipped to meet the needs of mature adults in the twenty-first century. And the definition of mature adults is changing. AARP defines seniors as those over fifty. One church I served has a seniors' group called "The Speeders—Over 55." The age that determines who is a senior is getting younger, and so are the seniors' lifestyles.

Today's society shatters *Webster's* traditional definition of retirement as a time of withdrawal or retreat. Myths and stereotypes associated with our maturing population are being exposed as false and misleading. More and more active adults, fifty-five and better, are embracing the trend toward a more healthy and active lifestyle, which extends beyond mere physical well-being.[4]

This book focuses on senior adult ministries within the local church. In this book, I explore the feelings and emotions of mature adults and demonstrate how the "graying" of the church can actually be a wonderful opportunity for the "growing of the church" in the twenty-first century.[5]

Senior adults are more than simply another group whose needs we must learn to meet. Many of these new senior adults, with their experiences and expertise, offer congregations incredible resources. We must encourage them to be vitally involved in local church ministry.

Local church ministry needs the experience and wisdom of mature adults. This book gives a step-by-step plan for establishing a senior adult ministry and ways in which mature adults can find fulfillment in the church.

My vision for this book is that it will serve as a handbook on effective ministry with mature adults. My hope is to sound an alarm, arousing congregations to awareness of the great opportunity for mature adult ministry for a new century. I provide principles and methodologies to accomplish the task of meeting senior adult needs for ministry.

My hope is that this collection of practical ideas, tools, and resources will lead you toward a successful ministry to senior adults.

CHAPTER 1

GETTING TO KNOW SENIOR ADULTS

It isn't true that as we age we become like everyone else. I've found, in fact, that as people mature, they become even more unique and individualistic. It's also a myth to think that senior adults contribute less as they age. Seniors volunteer more than any other age segment.

Today senior adults live longer, are more active, and are more creative than ever before. Almost one quarter of the average American's life will be spent in retirement. Today's senior adult is the first leisure class in United States history. Senior adults in the twenty-first century have a new face—the face of volunteerism.

Senior adults in the twenty-first century have a new face—the face of volunteerism.

THE NEW FACE OF SENIOR ADULTS

The profile of mature America has changed. Senior adults have more choices, more activities, and more friends than ever before. They live longer, happier lives than at any other time in our history. In fact, more than half of the disposable income in the United States is in the hands of those fifty-five and older.[1]

In previous years, I served two churches that were close to the beach in southern California. One of my favorite things to do in the evening was to walk along the beach and then sit on the lifeguard stand. I would watch the huge waves come in and crash against the shoreline. As we think about senior adult ministry, we must realize that the future really is an "age wave." Senior adults will provide a "flood" of opportunity for the church. Just to know about this phenomenon, however, "is no guarantee that a church will catch the wave. In fact, the possibility of most churches doing so is fairly remote, given the present set of attitudes, activities, and priorities."[2]

In the past, senior adults were thought of as requiring help; in this century, seniors will be those giving help. There comes a point in life when each of us will need specialized care, but for today's seniors, that point comes much later in life. For example, I was asked to go golfing with a friend (a senior) who had recently begun attending our church. We set the time at 2:00 p.m. When we met and exchanged greetings, I asked what he had been doing throughout the day. He told me that he had played tennis in the morning, followed by a light lunch with his wife. He was on a softball team and had played right up until 2:00 p.m., at which time he was now ready to play a round of golf with me. I was amazed! This vividly reinforced the fact that today's senior adults are alert, active, and energetic. Believe it or not, after our golf game, he asked me if he would see me at the fitness center that evening!

> **In the past, senior adults were thought of as requiring help; in this century, seniors will be those giving help.**

Today's seniors take computer classes and have multiple special interests. They enjoy not only motor homes and travel, but also motorcycling, rock climbing, and in-line skating. A monthly publication for the residents of the Sun City Grand, an age-restricted community on the outskirts of Phoenix, Arizona, features activities and interests of the senior adults living in that community. Listed in that one publication are Art Club, Book Review, Ceramics Club, Garden Club, Grand Stitchers, Photo/Video Club, R/C Flyers, Stained Glass Club, Woodcrafters, Motorcycling, R-Vers, Singles Club, Shalom Social Group, Travel Club, Bicycling, Billiards, Bocce Ball, Bowling, Dance, Golf, Lady Putters, Horseshoes, Hiking/Walking, Kayaking, Lawn Bowling, Mountain Biking, Roller Blading, Sailing, Scuba Diving, Softball, Swimming,

Tennis, Table Tennis, Water Polo, Drama/Comedy Club, Music Club, Dominoes, Scrabble, Bridge Club, Canasta, Cribbage, Pinochle, Poker, Computers, and the list goes on!

Seniors used to be thought of as care receivers; in the future they'll be caregivers. Nearly every senior I work with is involved in care-giving ministry. They volunteer at the local hospital, in service organizations, and in the church. Some are involved in hospice care, others at the library. Senior adults love to be helpful. They enjoy being involved and feeling needed. They want to see the results of their efforts.

In the past, most churches across America gave little attention to senior adult ministry. If we're to grow and follow Christ's command, we'll need to place a major focus on senior adult ministry in the future. Old stereotypes of seniors need to be discarded, and new images of active, vibrant, mature senior adults must come into focus. Rather than thinking of retirement as a slow-down time, we need to realize that retirement is the opportunity for people to devote time to learning, serving, planning, and living more active and exciting lives than they have ever lived before.

> **Rather than thinking of retirement as a slow-down time, we need to realize that retirement is the opportunity for people to devote time to learning, serving, planning, and living more active and exciting lives than they have ever lived before.**

Senior adults have a wealth of expertise and experience. They know much about our world and about biblical truth. That's why in this century we need to find creative ways of sharing God's love with seniors in relational ways. The focus must move from large lecture groups to smaller, caring fellowships that encourage involvement. In our ministry to senior adults, we must move from intellectual and biblical "facts" to application and experience. Seniors want to know what the Bible means for them today.

JUST WHO ARE THE SENIORS?

There is little consensus about who makes up the group we call seniors. As I mentioned in the introduction, AARP defines seniors as those over fifty. The Social Security Administration sees age sixty-five as the mark of being a senior.[3] Churches come up with all kinds of labels and standards by which they define seniors. Some churches use words like *elderly, senior citizens, silver circle,* or *golden-agers.* I've served in churches where more interesting names were used, such as "Speeders—Over 55," "Pacemakers," and "Friendship Class/Club."

Whatever the nomenclature, the term *senior adult* does not represent a numerical age or category. A twenty-first-century senior adult has more to do with attitude and lifestyle. Senior adults do not think of themselves as old, older, or declining. They view themselves as alive, vibrant, active, and moving forward to accomplish things they've always wanted but never had the time for.

There are some real contrasts among seniors. Some are quiet, soft, sweet, and flexible; others have become harsh, brittle, and cranky. Some have a great vision for the future, while others refuse to live for today and can only look in the past. Some enjoy active, healthy lives, while others seemingly suffer with pain and grief constantly. Some have material wealth, while others seem to be destined (or determined) to a life of poverty and loneliness. Some are growing spiritually, and others are stagnant and spiritually dry.

Senior adults are individuals.

Building an effective ministry to senior adults involves knowing the basic characteristics of seniors, in particular how they relate to the church and spirituality.

But that doesn't mean that there aren't some basic, age-appropriate characteristics common among seniors. Building an effective ministry to senior adults involves knowing the basic characteristics of seniors, in particular how they relate to the church and spirituality. What follows is a profile of active seniors that you should become intimately familiar with. It will help you navigate through what can be the choppy waters of senior adult ministry. More than just theory, these characteristics are things I've discovered in my real-life ministry to senior adults.

15 Characteristics of Active Senior Adults

See the characteristic response sheet on page 32 in the "Senior Adult Ministry Tools" section at the end of this chapter.

1. Senior adults love creative teaching. While seniors enjoy a traditional sermon, they also appreciate creative, thought-provoking discussions and involvement. I am the senior pastor in a church start that's only a few years old. Our church began with twenty-six in the core group. In just a few years, our membership has grown to three hundred, and it continues to grow weekly. Before coming to this new senior adult ministry, I served as pastor of a Midwestern church that had a 150-year history. I knew a lot about church traditions, and when I came to this senior adult church, I was expecting tradition to be equally important to these seniors. Not so! Yes, senior adults love stability and faithfulness, but they are surprisingly open to change. I have found that senior adults love creativity. In fact, many seniors were on the cutting edge of technology decades ago.

2. Senior adults love to be with friends; they need a warm, loving, and caring church family. Our church, Palm West Community Church, is called the "People Who Care Church." That's our theme. Nearly everything we do comes from that basic premise. On Sunday mornings our worship begins five minutes before the hour, specifically for the purpose of creating a warm, loving, and caring atmosphere. Greeters are at the doors, welcome signs are out, and ushers are ready with bulletins and friendly handshakes. More important, however, folks are shaking hands and hugging one another. As the senior pastor, I go from person to person, sharing warmth, love, and a caring attitude.

As the organ plays a prelude, the choir enters, and we're ready for worship. A hush falls on the sanctuary. As I welcome folks, friendship pads are passed out for everyone to indicate their attendance. This is not a meaningless weekly activity. On Monday morning the friendship pads are carefully checked for the specific purpose of finding out who was missing. Immediate follow-up is critical. Why is it so important? This

Senior adults love to be with friends; they need a warm, loving, and caring church family.

brings us back to our purpose, the "People Who Care" church. If we really do care, we notice when people are missing. We let those who were absent know they were missed, and we find out if anything is wrong.

After the friendship pads have been collected and some opportunities for Christian growth briefly pointed out, we continue to promote an attitude of warmth, love, and caring by inviting everyone to stand and express Christian greetings to one another. Senior adults love to be with friends; they need a warm, loving, and caring church family.

When I first came to this congregation, I was known as the "hugging pastor." It became almost humorous because nearly every Sunday, I had to take my suit to the cleaners because of makeup on my suit coat. One Sunday I announced that when I stood at the door, I would not have my suit coat on. It's less expensive to take a shirt to the cleaners than a suit! That simple statement brought many positive comments from our folks. They told their friends, "Our pastor really loves us." I also began having precious widows come to me at our evening service saying, "Pastor, I didn't get my hug this morning. Do I get two tonight?"

3. Senior adults love to sacrifice for a truly worthwhile project, goal, or cause. Senior adults know a lot about sacrifice. Many lived through the depression. Many have served in the armed forces. Many have lost loved ones. Most have

If a senior adult is shown a worth- while project, goal, or cause, he or she will almost always respond in a positive way.

experienced deep pain—physically, financially, and/or emotionally. They know what it means to sacrifice. If a senior adult is shown a worthwhile project, goal, or cause, he or she will almost always respond in a posi- tive way. What's important in senior ministry is to dif- ferentiate the various ways in which God blesses. Some are blessed with gifts of teaching, some with good health, and some with financial resources.

The Apostle Paul wrote about this in 1 Corinthians 12:1-12: "Now about spiritual gifts, brothers, I do not want you to be ignorant. You know that when you were pagans, somehow or other you were influenced and led astray to mute idols. Therefore I tell you that no one who is speaking by the Spirit of God says, 'Jesus be cursed,' and no one can say, 'Jesus is Lord,' except by the Holy Spirit. There are different kinds of gifts, but the same Spirit. There are different kinds of service, but the same Lord. There are different kinds of working, but the same God works all of them in all men. Now to each one the manifestation of the Spirit is given for the common good. To one there is given through the Spirit the message of wisdom, to another the message of knowledge by means of the same Spirit, to another faith by the same Spirit, to another gifts of healing by that one Spirit, to another miraculous powers, to another prophecy, to another distinguishing between spirits, to another speaking in different kinds of tongues, and to still another the interpretation of tongues. All these are the work of one and the same Spirit, and he gives them to each one, just as he determines. The body is a unit, though it is made up of many parts; and though all its parts are many, they form one body. So it is with Christ."

Senior adults love to sacrifice for a truly worthwhile project, goal, or cause. Whether it's involvement in short-term mission work, giving to special projects, or local outreach in the community, if challenged biblically, senior adults will rise to the challenge. They must see the project as worthwhile. They must sense the urgency of the need. They must feel that they, personally, will make a difference.

4. Senior adults love a caring pastor and staff. Actually, senior adults love caring leaders, period. Many years ago, I discovered the simple phrase, "As the leadership goes, so goes the church." That's to say, as the pastor goes, so goes the leadership; and as the leadership goes, so go the people. Show me an abrupt, remote, or aloof pastor, and chances are high that the leadership and people within the congregation will be much the same. A loving people are drawn to a loving pastor and leadership. People love a caring pastor and staff.

I have also observed that a great pastor makes a great church and a great church makes a great pastor.

Show me an abrupt, remote, or aloof pastor, and chances are high that the leadership and people within the congregation will be much the same.

The relationship is what is important. So often, young pastors leave seminary with their agenda, only to experience a lack of trust and an unwillingness to accept the many changes they try to initiate. Our top priorities are to love and care. Senior adults delight in being with and around a caring pastor and staff.

5. Senior adults love stability and predictability. In their many years, seniors have seen a lot. They've seen fads come and go. They've read the books, seen the videos, heard the seminar leaders; they've "been there, done that." Seniors are a "back to the basics" people. They enjoy creativity and challenge, but the bottom line is stability and predictability.

Changing the order of worship every Sunday is not helpful for senior adults. Constantly presenting new projects can be frustrating to them, to say the least. I have found that stability and predictability are essential needs of seniors. Paul wrote to the church at Corinth, "So then, men ought to regard us as servants of Christ and as those entrusted with the secret things of God. Now it is required that those who have been given a trust must prove faithful" (1 Corinthians 4:1-2). Mature adults, more than any other group in the church, are looking for faithfulness.

Mature adults, more than any other group in the church, are looking for faithfulness.

6. Senior adults want to associate with those of like beliefs and values. One of the wonderful blessings of the church is our common bond in Christ. I heard Bill Hybels speak a few years ago, and his theme was "There is nothing like the local church—when it is working right." As he spoke, he developed the thought that when the local church is functioning biblically, as God intends for it to function, there really is nothing else in the entire world quite so wonderful or so powerful. There is no place you would rather be. When the church is *not* working right, however, the damage can be brutal. Nearly every Christian can tell war stories that would bring tears to your eyes.

Seniors love to be with those of like faith. They love to sing the hymns of the church that they have sung for decades. They love to sing the praise and worship choruses that reflect their oneness in Christ. They love to sense the joy of biblical belief that determines their courses of action. They love to share in their common sense of biblical values. Senior adults love to associate with those of like beliefs and values.

7. Senior adults love to show respect to authority and to their rich heritage, and they feel saddened when they see these values lost. Patriotism and symbols like the flag are extremely important. So are patriotic holidays such as Memorial Day, Veteran's Day, and Independence Day. For church leaders, this is not only a characteristic of the twenty-first-century senior adult, but it also gives insight into how we can more effectively minister to these wonderful people.

If seniors love to show respect to authority and to their rich heritage, and they feel saddened when they see these values lost, that means they also have a tremendous respect for authority in the church and in the Christian heritage and Christian values. How refreshing!

When holidays come, it's important to give special recognition not only to the holidays, but also to the people whom the holidays honor. On Veteran's Day or the Sunday prior to Veteran's Day, during the worship service there could be special recognition of those who served in the armed forces. Encouraging people to wear uniforms and having special guests representing the various branches of the armed services are ways to help meet this need. Providing literature or writing an article in the church newsletter or the senior newsletter of the church is another way to highlight these special days.

Special days provide special opportunities for the church to meet these special needs of senior adults. Since seniors desire to be involved, and they have such a rich heritage, encourage individuals to share their experiences. "Ministry Moments," "Heritage Moments," or some other two-minute story presented during worship is a wonderful way to bring focus to these meaningful occasions.

Senior adults do love to show respect to authority. This is a huge plus for church leadership. Seniors desire to help leadership in any way possible. They have been there; they know the stresses of leadership. Not only can they sympathize with the pressures, but they can empathize with church leaders as well. Since senior adults have a rich heritage, they can share insights of wisdom. They've been in churches for decades and have seen what works and what doesn't. We may have a tendency to think that our senior adults are living in the past sometimes, but we need to remind ourselves that their past experiences can provide a wealth of wisdom for our future.

Seniors desire to help leadership in any way possible. They have been there; they know the stresses of leadership. Not only can they sympathize with the pressures, but they can empathize with church leaders as well.

Seniors also feel saddened when they see values lost. As we look around us today, nearly every newspaper, television, radio news program, or magazine reflects our culture's loss of biblical values. Churches that are meeting the needs of the seniors of the twenty-first century will be prepared to help senior adults cope with this changing world and will challenge them to help make a difference.

8. Senior adults accept change but prefer gradual change that has a meaningful purpose. Today's seniors are looking for meaningful purpose. Think about it. Senior adults have lived long lives. They've seen more changes than any other age group. They've seen good changes and bad changes. They've seen change merely for change's sake. They've seen changes that didn't work. As a result, it's natural that they would be somewhat skeptical when someone comes to present change.

If change is going to happen in a positive way, there must be careful and prayerful thought and time given to it.

That's why change must be done gradually. If change is going to happen in a positive way, there must be careful and prayerful thought and time given to it. Change involves risk, insecurity, and vulnerability for the leaders as well as for lay leadership. I have found that in order to make a change successfully, there are five things you should be sure of.

First, be sure the change meets a need. If change is simply for change's sake, seniors will not readily accept or adjust to the change. Changing the order of worship simply for change's sake will not cut it. If there's a need, however, change will be accepted. Be aware. Not everyone will sense the same need. For example, my preaching style is expository in nature. I am more a teacher than a preacher. When I arrived as pastor, after six or eight months, some folks asked for an outline (which I had used in previous churches but was careful not to push on this new congregation). Since there was a readiness on the part of some, I put the outline in the bulletin. Others, however, were not ready for that change. In order to meet the needs of both groups, the simple solution was to place the outlines next to the bulletins on a table in the foyer. Those who wanted them could simply pick one up when they arrived Sunday morning. When change is implemented, it must meet a need.

Second, be sure those involved in the change understand the potential consequences for themselves and others. Changing rooms, furniture, schedules, and programs impacts not only those directly involved, but also nearly everyone in the congregation. A change for one class or group directly affects those in other locations. And believe me, word travels fast among senior adults! To make positive change, we must understand the consequences for others as well as ourselves.

Third, make sure seniors believe that the change can be accomplished. This may take time. It's one thing to demonstrate a need; it is quite another to show that the change can be accomplished. Short-term mission projects are wonderful, but for seniors who have never traveled, they may seem totally impossible. "Baby steps" become important. Begin with what your senior group *can* do, then gradually move on to bigger steps that will be a challenge to them.

Fourth, make sure that seniors believe the change is better than what they already have. If things are comfortable now, why change? That seems logical to anyone. It's important to conduct careful and prayerful planning, to show practical reasons why the change is needed. This does not happen overnight.

Finally, make sure you involve seniors in the process of change. Simply making the change and then announcing it will create havoc and incur bad feelings. Involving seniors in the process and allowing adequate time for adjustment will bring lasting results.

9. Senior adults love institutions and organizations that have touched their lives in the past. When you think of mature senior adults, you have to think of their history. They've attended universities and graduate schools. In years past, they've been honored by organizations and institutions for which they've worked, served, and had allegiance. When you visit seniors in their homes, they'll quickly show you a wall on which are plaques and trophies from special events and organizations. Take note of these important memories; they'll help you connect with seniors' pasts.

I conducted a funeral of a man who had been a recipient of a gold medal in the Olympics. As the family showed me the medal and began to explain a very humorous incident, I could not help but connect with this wonderful man. Apparently, he was standing on a dock following an Olympic event. The athletes were lined up, standing solemnly as they awaited their medals. This man somehow allowed the gold medal to slip through his hands! It fell through the crack of the dock, and when they came to place it over his head, he had to explain that he had dropped it.

Whether it's their country, a place of former employment, or some place they served as a volunteer, seniors love institutions and organizations that have touched their lives. How does this impact the church and senior adult ministry? Seniors who have been involved in their churches over the years love their churches. Many have moved to new communities and, sadly, have not found new church homes. They're looking for new connections that will provide stability and comfort during times of need. The local church must become one of those very special "institutions" or communities that touch the lives of senior adults.

> **The local church must become one of those very special "institutions" or communities that touch the lives of senior adults.**

10. Senior adults love to show loyalty beyond description. Seniors are loyal in their marriages, their churches, their clubs, and their organizations. Loyalty is a stalwart staple in senior adult ministry. Yet there is a paradox in this characteristic. Seniors are loyal beyond description; however, they have a crossover point. If they feel that their needs are not being met, they'll begin to search for a community of believers in which their needs will be met.

Without question, senior adult ministry is time-consuming. Constant follow-up is extremely important. You cannot allow seniors to be missing from your ministry without immediate follow-up. Telephone calls, postcards, and personal visits are musts. When you demonstrate your loyalty to seniors, they in turn show loyalty beyond description to you, to the church, and to Christ.

11. Senior adults love to volunteer, to serve, and to give. The list of ways in which seniors can volunteer is limitless. If seniors are not involved in the local church, they'll offer their services everywhere and anywhere. You'll be surprised to see your own seniors serving throughout the community when you've neglected to use them in the local church. Seniors will be found volunteering in every conceivable organization. They'll volunteer in various health care facilities, foster care facilities, protective service agencies, Alzheimer's care centers, American Legion, various clubs, and support groups. They'll volunteer at museums, Big Brothers/Big Sisters, YMCA, blood banks, Chamber of Commerce, charitable organizations, counseling programs, country clubs, local law enforcement agencies, elder care, food/meal programs, nursing homes, Salvation Army, senior programs, and scores of other organizations—but not your local congregation. You name it, seniors will be found helping. There's nothing wrong with seniors helping nonchurch organizations, unless they're doing so because they don't feel needed in their local church.

Ephesians 4:11-13 gives the biblical plan for ministry: "It was he who gave some to be apostles, some to be prophets, some to be evangelists, and some to be pastors and teachers, to prepare God's people for works of service, so that the body of Christ may be built up until we all reach unity in the faith and in the knowledge of the Son of God and become mature, attaining to the whole measure of the fullness of Christ."

It's clear that God has given gifts to all believers in order that they may do the work of ministry so that the body of Christ might be built up. It's our responsibility as leaders in the church of the twenty-first century to follow the biblical mandate: Equip the believers so they may do the work of ministry, in order that the body of Christ is built up. This means that the local church in general, and senior adult ministry in particular, must become a

As we teach and equip our senior adults to do ministry, it's important to also be a healing community.

teaching/equipping center. As we teach and equip our senior adults to do ministry, it's important to also be a healing community. The byproduct of teaching/equipping and healing is that our seniors will be a responding family and a deploying agency. This deploying, or reaching out, will be discussed in Chapter 4.

12. Senior adults love to talk and share their feelings and experiences. We joke about older folks liking to talk, but as you think about it, they do have a lot to talk about. This means that lecture is not the only way for teaching. Actually, in working with seniors, I have found just the opposite to be true. Here are ten ways to help seniors enjoy learning as *they* talk and share their feelings and experiences:

- *Encourage seniors to explore and discover biblical truth for themselves.* For seniors, learning is greatly enhanced as they explore and discover the personal meaning of events and ideas.

For seniors, learning is greatly enhanced as they explore and discover the personal meaning of events and ideas.

- *Allow differences of opinion.* Difference is good. Difference is actually desirable. Difference allows for creativity. Remember that God created each of us to be unique. Senior adults have so much to share from their rich history. This is especially true when you have seniors who have come from many different parts of the country or the world. Rather than true/false statements or questions, try using some agree/disagree statements or questions. You may be surprised at how involved your senior adults will get in the discussion.

- *Encourage involvement.* Instead of lecturing, try activities and discussions in which your seniors are "doing" rather than listening.

- *Allow for mistakes.* Actually, it's the learner's right to make mistakes. That is one way we learn. In discussions, accept all responses in nonjudgmental ways. Phrases such as "That is one thought" and "I never really thought of it in that way" help create open thinking and discussion where mistakes and differences of thought can be accepted.

Ambiguity is another important part of allowing for mistakes. Your seniors may not always have all the right answers, nor should they. Sometimes seniors wrestle with thoughts, concepts, and ideas, and they become very unclear and ambiguous. That is not only acceptable, but it is a healthy part of learning.

- *Allow for cooperation and collaboration in learning.* This reinforces the fact that we need one another. None of us have all the answers. Together we study Scripture, and God through the Holy Spirit is our teacher. Ecclesiastes 4:9 says, "Two are better than one, because they have a good return for their work."

- *Encourage openness and transparency.* There are too many places in our society that create concealment and dishonesty. Where else but in the church, the body of Christ, may we be open, honest, accepting, and transparent? Lead by example in this area.

- *Help seniors feel accepted.* Nothing will chase a visitor away more quickly than feeling left out or not accepted. Most of the discontentment in today's senior adult ministries is due to the fact that someone felt unaccepted. Create feelings of acceptance within your senior adult ministry.

- *Encourage respect.* Respect is crucial for all age groups, but seniors expect respect at this point in their lives. Without respect, you may be teaching, but there may not be learning. Respect comes from a lifestyle. Respect is a result of attitudes that have been created. You respect your seniors, and they'll respect each other.

- *Focus on the personal application for the lives of your senior adults.* It's of little help to know lists of facts without practical personal application. This leads to the final way to help seniors learn integration of biblical facts.

- *Use integration of biblical facts and life application.* Integrating the biblical facts into life is perhaps the most important key for learning among seniors. Seniors must put into practice the biblical content they are learning.

Integrating the biblical facts into life is perhaps the most important key for learning among seniors. Seniors must put into practice the biblical content they are learning.

13. Senior adults love to be busy. If health permits it, they are on the go, filled with energy. Senior adults have spurts of energy. When their health is good, they want to be active. Their activity may be brief, but it's important to allow seniors to keep busy within the church family. One of the most helpful innovations I have found is when I created a "pastoral assistance team." This team has been invaluable in my ministry with senior adults, and a suggested job description is in the "Senior Adult Ministry Tools" section at the end of this chapter (p. 30). The purpose of such a team is to assist by discovering spiritual gifts in laypersons and then recruiting, training, equipping, coordinating, and placing in service those persons to do the work of ministry.

The basic duties of the pastoral assistance team coordinator center on discovering spiritual gifts in laypersons. The position is created specifically to help laypersons use their spiritual gifts for service to the Lord. This team will make hospital visits and sit with family members of a loved one during the loved one's surgery. The team makes visits to homebound members and friends and serves communion to them once each month.

We have a coffee time in our home every other week, and this team has someone who lines up people to attend the "coffee time with the pastor." A pastoral assistance team is a tremendous source of energy and encouragement.

14. Senior adults love to share their faith in simple relational ways. In Chapter 4 we'll look at specific ways to help your senior adults reach out to others. At this point, it's enough to say that seniors love to share their faith in simple, relational ways. Most seniors enjoy chatting with friends. As opportunities arise, if equipped, they're more than willing to share their faith in a simple, warm, and personal way with friends and neighbors.

> Most seniors enjoy chatting with friends. As opportunities arise, if equipped, they're more than willing to share their faith in a simple, warm, and personal way with friends and neighbors.

15. Senior adults love children, youth, and young adults. They intensely love their families, especially their grandchildren. It goes without saying that seniors love to be with children (for brief periods of time!). One of the humorous statements we often hear is how much grandparents love having their children and grandchildren come over to visit, especially when they can spoil the grandkids and then give them back to the parents. We laugh, but it's true. Seniors love children, youth, and young adults and want to help in various ways on limited-time bases. It's important for the church of the twenty-first century to utilize the wealth of wisdom and resources of senior adults in helping with children, youth, and young adults.

WHAT ABOUT LESS ACTIVE SENIOR ADULTS?

Up to this point, we've focused on active senior adults. The previous fifteen characteristics reflect the seniors you may be working with who are alert, energetic, and active in their lifestyles. However, there are seniors who are homebound or in need of either short- or long-term care. It's important that you consider their characteristics as well.

Long life spans and changing living patterns have made the later senior years a new and somewhat uncharted adventure.

Advances in health care have made living with disabilities and caregiving in the later years of life both a reality and a challenging responsibility. There are many options of care available today in all parts of the country.[4] It's important that leaders in the church of the twenty-first century become familiar with the options available.

Use the following check list of activities of daily living to help determine if the individual is independent, needs help to perform a task, or is unable to do so at all:

	Yes	No
Walking: Can the individual move about with or without devices or help from another person?	☐	☐
Transferring: Can he change positions from bed to chair to toilet without assistance?	☐	☐

	Yes	No

Bathing: Can she get to the bathroom, prepare hot water, get into the tub or shower, and wash unassisted? .... ☐ ... ☐

Dressing and Grooming: Can the individual dress without assistance, put on artificial limbs or braces, and perform grooming tasks such as washing hair or shaving? .... ☐ ... ☐

Medicine: Can she reliably take the correct medication at the proper time? .... ☐ ... ☐

Eating: Can he feed himself? .... ☐ ... ☐

Housekeeping: Can the individual do minimal cleaning in the house and do the laundry? .... ☐ ... ☐

Telephone: Can he use the telephone to communicate with others or to request help? .... ☐ ... ☐

Food Preparation: Can she prepare or heat meals? .... ☐ ... ☐

Security: Can the individual exercise care in locking windows and doors? .... ☐ ... ☐

Toileting: Can he get to the bathroom and use all of the facilities? .... ☐ ... ☐

Shopping: Can she plan and prepare meals and also do the necessary grocery shopping? .... ☐ ... ☐

Communication of Needs: Can the individual make needs and desires known by any means of communication? ...... ☐ ... ☐

Safety: Can she recognize and correct hazardous conditions in the home? .... ☐ ... ☐

Orientation: Is he accurately aware of places, people, days and years? .... ☐ ... ☐

Decision Making: Can the individual make appropriate choices? .... ☐ ... ☐

Medical Needs: Are there conditions that would require skilled nursing care? .... ☐ ... ☐

Nighttime Care: Can the individual be left alone at night and can he call for help if needed? .... ☐ ... ☐

Scoring: If you answered NO on 15 questions or more, this may be an indication of the need for 24 hour care such as skilled care, supervisory care or assisted living care.

If you answered NO on 7 or more questions, this may indicate the need for in-home or out of home supportive services such as adult day health care, respite service or home companions, or in-home homemakers, health aides.

If you want help in evaluating the patient and family needs, a variety of resources are available for help.

- Hospital discharge plans should be discussed with the social services department of the hospital. They can make recommendations and will assist in the implementation of the care needed.
- The case manager…can evaluate needs and arrange for the provision of needed services.
- Nurses employed by home health agencies may assist the individual and/or the caregiver in evaluation and arranging for needed help.

Once strengths and problems are identified, you can begin to match needs with available long and short term care services.

If the activities of daily living can be managed independently, the choice may be to: Remain in the present home with the help of…support services…

If you discover that more specialized services are needed, the decision might be to: Remain in the present home and make use of home health care services. These might include nursing care, home health aides, and therapists…

Even with these kinds of help, remaining at home may not be possible. If some protection, supervision or help with daily activities is needed, the best solution might be to: Change residence to a supervisory care home where room, board and supervision are provided. Such homes require a resident to be able to care for themselves and to get around without help…

If more assistance and 24 hour supervision is recommended, it may be desirable to consider residence in an adult care home.

If health problems or disabilities require around the clock nursing care, the best decision might be to: Change residence to a health care center (nursing home) where 24 hour nursing and rehabilitation services are provided…

Socialization in a supervised setting can make a long illness less trying for a family. Adult day care provides professionally supervised recreation, socialization, nutrition and health supervision. In assisting families adult day care can help prevent premature or inappropriate institutionalization. Respite is provided for caregivers allowing them to pursue necessary shopping and errand activities while their family member enjoys a safe and stimulating environment.

Hospice services are available both in-home and in dedicated facilities during a final illness. Because of the pioneering work of Cicely Saunders, a compassionate physician in England, the last months of life need not be spent in isolation, pain and fear. Sensitive volunteers and professionals can provide care and support through hospice services licensed by the State. When services are given by a Medicare approved hospice, the costs are covered for 100% through the Medicare hospice benefit.

It is helpful for [church leaders working with senior adults] to know the distinction between various types of long and short term care...

Home health agencies which are state licensed and are Medicare certified provide periodic nursing care, as needed, and at least one other service in the home. Care is given only under a physician's direction. A specific plan of treatment is written for each person. Qualified nurses and therapists provide or supervise the care.

In addition to nursing care, home health agencies provide one or more of the following services:

- *Home Health Aide:* Homemaker service and/or help with one's personal care.
- *Physical Therapy:* Supervised exercise, treatment, training and education to renew or increase physical abilities.
- *Occupational Therapy:* Supervised exercises and other activities to renew or increase the ability to perform daily living tasks such as dressing, eating, homemaking and leisure activities.
- *Speech Therapy:* Supervised activities to renew or increase speech and language abilities.
- *Medical Social Service:* Counseling individuals and their families to help them in adjusting to physical and emotional problems.

- *Nutritional Counseling:* Information on nutritional care, special diets, meal times and food management.[5]

There are also adult care homes, supervisory care homes, and health care centers (nursing homes). Normally, health care centers offer three levels of nursing care: personal care, skilled care, and sub-acute care.[6]

Getting to know what seniors are like is foundational to a successful senior adult ministry. I strongly encourage you to go back over this chapter and reflect on your own seniors' group. Use this chapter's ministry tool pages that follow to begin to apply these foundational concepts to your ministry situation. The better you understand seniors, the more likely you'll be able to minister in a way that brings about significant life change.

The better you understand seniors, the more likely you'll be able to minister in a way that brings about significant life change.

PASTORAL ASSISTANCE TEAM COORDINATOR
(OR ASSOCIATE PASTOR)
JOB DESCRIPTION

PURPOSE:

To assist the senior pastor by discovering spiritual gifts in laypersons and then recruiting, training, equipping, coordinating, and placing in service those persons to do the work of ministry at [name of your church].

"It was he who gave some to be apostles, some to be prophets, some to be evangelists, and some to be pastors and teachers, to prepare God's people for works of service, so that the body of Christ may be built up until we all reach unity in the faith and in the knowledge of the Son of God and become mature, attaining to the whole measure of the fullness of Christ" (EPHESIANS 4:11-13).

DUTIES:

The basic duties of the pastoral assistance team coordinator (or associate pastor) center on discovering spiritual gifts in laypersons. The duties involve recruiting, training, equipping, coordinating, and placing in service laypersons to assist with pastoral ministry. The position is created specifically to help laypersons use their spiritual gifts for service to the Lord. In so doing, the associate pastor needs to place into service laypersons who will...

1. make hospital visits on Saturday, Sunday, and Monday as requested by the senior pastor.

2. sit with family members of a loved one during his or her surgery. The senior pastor will make a pastoral visit and pray with the person having surgery prior to the surgery. Laypersons will sit with family and friends during the surgery, and the senior pastor will make a return pastoral visit following surgery.

3. make Friday morning visits (coordinating Friday morning teams of two going out to make visits from 8:30 a.m. to noon):

   • to homebound members and friends. Weekly visits with the senior pastor to serve communion to homebound members and friends, making sure that all homebound, shut-in members and friends receive communion once each month.

   • to members and friends with special needs. Other teams of two going out to visit members and friends with special needs—such as missing from worship, recovering from surgery, experienced loss—as assigned by the senior pastor.

4. make weekly telephone calls. Obtain updates for the weekly prayer list, and report the updates to the administrative secretary by Thursday morning each week.

5. line up people to attend the "coffee time with the pastor" twice monthly. The senior pastor will provide the list of those in the congregation who have not yet been to his or her home.

6. line up the pastor's Thursday afternoon visits to first-time visitors. The senior pastor and his or her spouse visit from 1:00 to 5:00 each Thursday afternoon.

7. work with the shepherd group coordinator. Ensure a strong and healthy small group ministry in the congregation.

8. involve retired pastors within the congregation by inviting them to make visits, serve communion with the senior pastor to homebound members and friends, and coordinate a quarterly retired pastors' lunch.

9. The pastoral assistance team coordinator (or associate pastor) also will line up retired pastors in the congregation to make professional pastoral visits two days each week on Wednesdays and Thursdays. The senior pastor will make visits most days, but specifically on Tuesdays and Fridays.

SENIOR ADULT CHARACTERISTIC RESPONSE SHEET

Characteristic	Why this is significant	What we can do in our own senior adult ministry to help meet the need
1. Love creative teaching.		
2. Love to be with other friends, and love a warm caring church.		
3. Love to sacrifice for worthwhile project, goal, or cause.		
4. Love a caring pastor.		
5. Love stability and predictability.		
6. Love to associate with those of like beliefs and values.		
7. Love to show respect to authority and have a rich heritage.		
8. Love change if gradual and has meaningful purpose.		
9. Love institutions and organizations that have touched their lives.		
10. Love to show loyalty.		
11. Love to volunteer, serve, and give.		
12. Love to talk and share their feelings.		
13. Love to be busy if health permits.		
14. Love to share their faith in simple, relational ways.		
15. Love children, youth, and young adults.		

SENIOR ADULTS IN THE CHURCH TODAY

Agree   Disagree

1. Senior adults can learn as much by observing and listening as they can by participating (doing) and discussing. . . . . ☐ . . . ☐

2. The needs and problems of senior adults today are so different from middle-aged adults that these two groups should be in separate classes (groups). . . . . ☐ . . . ☐

3. In learning, you won't see changes in outward behavior or even in knowledge until there has been an attitude change. . . . . ☐ . . . ☐

4. It is better not to expect seniors to learn as much or as fast as other age groups. . . . . ☐ . . . ☐

5. Attitudes and beliefs of senior adults are really no more difficult to change than those of youth or children. . . . . ☐ . . . ☐

6. Seniors are more content to sit and listen than to engage in discussion and research. . . . . ☐ . . . ☐

7. More learning will occur if the classroom atmosphere allows differences of opinion or disagreement. ☐ . . . ☐

8. The teachers of senior adult classes should be allowed to select the courses and materials that they teach since they probably know the needs of their students better than others do. . . . . ☐ . . . ☐

9. Single senior adults can be integrated into couples or married senior adult classes as long as they are in the same age bracket. . . . . ☐ . . . ☐

10. In considering curriculum, uniform lessons (everyone in the entire adult program studies the same lesson) have more advantages than other types of programs such as classes choosing their own course of study and electives. . . . . ☐ . . . ☐

11. For all practical purposes, an adult class of sixty members is just as functional as one of thirty members. . . . . ☐ . . . ☐

12. In helping adults learn, they must have correct information or knowledge first before you can change their behavior or attitudes. . . ☐ . . . ☐

13. In senior ministry, men's classes should be separated from women's classes. . . . . ☐ . . . ☐

14. It is best to organize the senior adult classes by age rather than needs and interests. . . . . ☐ . . . ☐

PLAN FOR CHANGE IN OUR SENIOR ADULT MINISTRY

Some areas in which improvements are needed in my life	Obstacles blocking these	Steps to overcome these	Dates I will take these steps

CHAPTER 2

GETTING STARTED IN SENIOR ADULT MINISTRY

Senior adult ministry reminds me of the story about a granddaughter who was sitting on her grandpa's lap as he was reading the paper. Grandpa wasn't paying any attention to his granddaughter's study of the wrinkles on his old face. The sweet little girl got up the nerve to rub her fingers over his wrinkles. She then ran her fingers over her own face and looked very puzzled. Finally, she asked, "Grandpa, did God make you?" "God sure did, honey, a long time ago," he replied. "Well, did God make me?" she asked. "Yes, and that wasn't too long ago," he said. She thought for a moment and then said, "Boy! God sure is doing a lot better job these days."

God is allowing us to do a better job in our senior adult ministry these days. Contrary to what many may think, senior adult ministry is exciting. I have served in full-time ministry over the past thirty-five years in both large and small churches. I have never had more fun than in my current ministry as senior pastor of a church of all senior adults. I have spent many years working with children, youth, and young adults. During those years of happy ministry, I never realized the untapped potential, challenges, excitement, and satisfaction of working with seniors.

A few years ago, when two denominational leaders asked me to consider a new church working exclusively with senior adults, it sounded intriguing to me. Every member and friend in our congregation is a senior adult. An exciting challenge awaited me. And I love a challenge!

We're called to help all people, including mature adults, achieve the highest possible level of the abundant life Jesus came to offer.

The church in the twenty-first century has a responsibility to help and care for senior adults. We're called to help all people, including mature adults, achieve the highest possible level of the abundant life Jesus came to offer (John 10:10). While the church is primarily concerned with the spiritual, it is impossible to separate the spiritual from the other aspects of life. Senior adults need the attention of our ministry efforts, as do other age groups under our care.

Churches could be doing a better job ministering to senior adults as we move into the twenty-first century. We could be meeting the needs and interests of the senior adults in our congregations and in our communities in fresh, creative ways. We could be releasing them to plan and direct their own ministries. Seniors are fully capable adults who are able to navigate their own lives and ministries. As we find innovative ways to release them into ministry, they'll rediscover the joy of being members of the body of Christ.

Seniors are fully capable adults who are able to navigate their own lives and ministries. As we find innovative ways to release them into ministry, they'll rediscover the joy of being members of the body of Christ.

THE NEED FOR THE CHURCH TO RESPOND

The church must be concerned with the whole person. Seniors look to the church to assist them in meeting both spiritual and functional needs. To help meet all the needs of a senior, every church should consider the following responses:

- While recognizing basic needs of older persons, we must take into consideration spiritual health and growth.
- While acknowledging the need to stimulate the mind and provide opportunities to expand senior adults' information and skills, we must consider providing continual learning.

- While realizing that an important function of the church is to provide Christian fellowship, we must consider providing social interaction.
- While providing for our senior adults' need to continue to be useful, as well as the church's need for volunteers in ministry, we must consider service opportunities.
- We must consider providing services to meet the needs of senior adults that they cannot meet for themselves.
- We must consider a wide variety of ministries *to* senior adults, from pastoral ministries to social services.
- We must consider ministry *for* senior adults, providing help on behalf of our seniors, which may take the form of advocacy. This also includes those provisions the church makes in its regular programming for all ages, such as Bible study groups, worship, and fellowship activities.
- We must consider that people in their retirement years, as a segment of the population, have more discretionary financial resources than any other age group and that their disposition to donate to worthy causes is greater than that of all other age groups. Stewardship of time, talent, and resources is an important part of senior adult ministry.

---

9 BENEFITS OF ESTABLISHING A SENIOR ADULT MINISTRY

There are many benefits of having a strong senior adult ministry in your church. Consider the following:

Young families are looking for a church that will meet the needs of Mom and Dad and Grandma and Grandpa.

1. *Senior adult ministry expands the church's existing ministry by reaching entire families, including grandparents and homebound seniors.* If you minister to Grandma and Grandpa, you have touched the lives of their children and grandchildren. Children and grandchildren are impressed when they see a church that has an effective senior adult ministry. Friends tell friends, and good news travels fast. Young families are looking for a church that will meet the needs of Mom and Dad and Grandma and Grandpa.

2. *Senior adult ministry shows the community that the church is a vital part of community life.* Society is trying to meet the needs of senior adults. The church has waited too long to respond to these needs. Churches can be a more vital part of community life by providing senior activities, meals, trips, and social events.

3. *Senior adult ministry builds the Sunday school.* Seniors can touch the lives of children, grandchildren, and great-grandchildren. The young adults keep seniors active and alive, while the seniors give wisdom to the younger people in the church through Sunday school.

4. *Senior adult ministry increases worship attendance.* Families prefer to worship together. When seniors become interested in a social activity and become involved in the seniors group, it is likely that they'll begin participating in the worship service. Soon their families may join them. Interest in the church may lead to involvement; senior involvement may lead to regular membership.

Today's senior adults face issues such as media impact, loneliness, depression, fear, crime and violence, suicide, and alcohol abuse. The Bible provides guidelines for living and help for emotional hurts.

5. *Senior adult ministry instills biblical truth in the lives of seniors and helps them face the challenges of today's deteriorating society.* The issues facing families today, especially seniors, are horrendous. Today's senior adults face issues such as media impact, loneliness, depression, fear, crime and violence, suicide, and alcohol abuse. The Bible provides guidelines for living and help for emotional hurts. Churches can help seniors grow spiritually by applying biblical truth to their unique needs.

6. *Senior adult ministry provides enriching experiences close to home.* Senior adult networks can be established. Friendship groups, social events, and prayer groups all enrich the senior's life and are close to home—his or her own local church home.

7. *Senior adult ministry helps meet the need for senior care.* Seniors need stability, friendships, and relationships. Many seniors, however, find themselves left sitting alone in front of a television. Churches with effective senior adult ministries can provide food for the homebound, have a system in place to help provide transportation, and offer counseling services.

8. *Senior adult ministry provides an opportunity for mature adults to serve.*

Senior adults have so much to offer. They especially like to work with children. However, be careful not to overwork them. Even though seniors may always be available, plan and schedule their volunteer time, and stick to it.

Even though seniors may always be available, plan and schedule their volunteer time, and stick to it.

9. *Senior adult ministry provides an opportunity for young adults to serve.* Younger adults can help guide seniors in learning new skills. Young adults can teach computer classes or help seniors in physical fitness or exercise classes. Of course, this can work in the opposite direction as well—seniors teaching/serving young adults.

5 THINGS TO CONSIDER BEFORE STARTING A SENIOR ADULT MINISTRY

There is a ministry tool handout on page 55 related to these five things.

I have discovered some simple, practical, and effective steps in establishing a senior adult ministry:

1. Pray. Seek God's will in prayer, and share your prayerful concern and vision with others. Pray weekly with interested people. It has been said that often the first and only thing that will work is the last thing we try—prayer. It's important to seek God in any venture, especially one as important as senior adult ministry in the local church.

2. Count the cost. Luke 14:28 says, "Suppose one of you wants to build a tower. Will he not first sit down and estimate the cost to see if he has enough money to complete it?" Building a senior adult ministry will cost you and your congregation time, money, and emotions. Are you willing to pay the price?

Building a senior adult ministry will cost you and your congregation time, money, and emotions. Are you willing to pay the price?

One part of the cost involves problem solving. Seniors can have a lot of fun and good times, but there may also be conflict. Seniors may disagree and can be strong-willed. A few can even be highly critical, negative, and cranky. I once knew a senior adult who simply could not be pleased. Two things I remember about him: He didn't like one particular pastoral staff person, and he didn't want change. One weekend when we had a major training event scheduled, to which the entire community was invited, he asked me who all of the people were. When I told him that we had invited them to our training event, his response was simply, "Tell them that this is not their church and they should go home." He was serious. Thankfully, I was able to persuade him that we couldn't do that.

I also remember receiving a little note about an associate pastor on staff. A senior adult was critical of the way that pastor had led in worship the previous week. The note read, "We are not alone in this request for there are many good members in the church who are suffering also because of this staff member [and he wrote out the associate pastor's name]. One lady said she could scream when he is in the pulpit to open the services, as he prays and he cannot keep his hands off of his glasses. Last Sunday morning while praying, he fingered his glasses twenty-two times in a few minutes. Please send him back where he came from if they will have him, as we do not need him in this church."

These two examples are extreme, of course, but in every congregation in which I have served, I have found one or two members who provide such examples.

J. Oswald Sanders, in his book *Spiritual Leadership*, wrote, "No leader is exempt from criticism, and his [or her] humility will nowhere be seen more clearly than in the manner in which he [or she] accepts and reacts to it."[1]

> **Build a basis for mutual problem solving by realizing that you both share a commitment to ministry. You both have a vested interest in the outcome of the decision.**

I read a little quip about a certain village where somebody took the liberty of adding to the sign on the outskirts of the town: "Population 500—1 grouch."

Unfortunately, in most congregations there is one grouch—one person who complains constantly, one person who always sees the dark side of things. Learning to love, care for, and minister to that one grouch—along with the many happy, positive people—is part of counting the cost. In Chapter 3 there is a deeper look at dealing with criticism, but for now let me remind you to be ready for criticism and learn how to deal with it.

I have found in working with seniors that the real problem is not the issue (such as scheduling or programming). The real problem is the relationship between the persons involved. Build a basis for mutual problem solving by realizing that you both share a commitment to ministry. You both have a vested interest in the outcome of the decision. Remember that conflict is inherent in life, and there is a creative solution to every problem.

I have discovered five basic approaches to conflict. If used to increase awareness of coping with style (yours as well as others'), you can avoid many serious conflicts. (You may use the ministry tool handout on page 56 to evaluate the style of dealing with conflict within your church.)

a) *Surrender:* Seniors who avoid conflict will give in but possibly harbor resentment.

b) *Subversion:* The mother of the sons of Zebedee used this method with Jesus in Matthew 20:20-21. She went behind the other disciples' backs to try to get her way. It will not take you long in working with seniors to find out that some seniors are incredibly strong-willed and will go to the extreme to get their own way.

c) *Open warfare:* Arm yourself! If these seniors don't get their way, the whole church will know about it. And your job will be a miserable one. In many churches seniors have been there the longest. They often have many relatives in the congregation and sometimes have a great deal of financial influence. This is an issue for sensitivity, wisdom, prayer, and love.

d) *Adjustment:* Someone may decide that his or her part of the conflict is just not worth holding on to. As a result, that person will change to accommodate the other person. This can be unhealthy. Seniors have a tendency to give in outwardly but could hold a grudge inwardly. Love is the key here. Time must be spent with them. Countless hours may be required in working toward a positive solution. Remember, sometimes the best solution may be that someone steps down or even leaves a church for the overall good of the entire congregation.

e) *Negotiation:* This is the healthiest form of coping. The result of this strategy is that both parties arrive at and accept a solution to the problem. Remember that you have a tremendous responsibility to model healthy coping skills for church members. Remember, too, that senior adults who are "mature adults" have a tremendous responsibility to model healthy coping skills for younger people in the church. As leadership goes, so goes the group.

When you do not agree, you have three choices: Through anger, you may take a step against another person; through fear, you may take a step away from the other person; or through love, you may take a step toward the other person. In Ephesians 4:2, the Apostle Paul wrote, "Be completely humble and gentle; be patient, bearing with one another in love."

Some helpful suggestions for working with seniors on problem solving steps include:

• *Ask good questions.* When conflicts arise, ask yourself some of these questions: Why does this threaten me? Can I learn or benefit from this? Would I profit from changing? Is this attitude, belief, or behavior actually detrimental to the growth of our seniors' group or our relationship? Does my resistance to this conflict or change reflect the fruit of the Spirit in Galatians 5? Is my behavior what I want to model for others in our seniors' group?

• *Build relationships.* Focus on more than "business as usual" with seniors. Spend time together praying and having fun. Weekly prayer brings people together like nothing else. Playing together enables you to see other sides of each other. Cultivate friendships that will provide fun social times. Take a different person out to lunch each week. Express an interest in their personal lives. One example I've found helpful is to have small groups of seniors come to my home for a meal. The first week of each month, we had a brunch at 10:00 a.m. The second week of the month, we had a lunch at noon. The third week we had a dinner. Menus were planned for each meal, so the same simple meal was served (each brunch was the same, each lunch was the same, each dinner was the same). Folks could sign up for not only the time slot they liked, but also the type of meal they enjoyed. Everyone would sit around the table for an hour or so, eating and visiting, and then the group moved into the living room for simple discussion and fellowship.

• *Keep perspective.* Stressful relationships, especially with senior adults, can dim your view of the big picture. I keep a running list of what I call "Milestones and Roadblocks," noting major accomplishments and setbacks in my ministry. When I find myself discouraged, simply reading over the list of milestones encourages me. It's amazing how looking at the whole picture changes my perspective. We take a lot of pictures. It's fun to look through photo albums of the various social events or activities to reflect on how the senior ministry has grown.

• *Take care of details.* Thinking through the little things prevents many conflicts. A summary sheet of all income and expenses is important to a business administrator. A master list of everyone going on a seniors' trip with contact telephone numbers helps the church staff answer questions. Cleanup assigned ahead of time will make the custodian smile. If you keep the business administrator, the church secretary, and the custodian happy, you'll be blessed with many favors in return.

Thinking through the little things prevents many conflicts.

• *Know church policies.* Know what is appropriate and what is not. Read through the church constitution, all policy books, and handbooks to learn church policies. Glance through all church board minutes once a month. Know how the key leaders feel about issues. If you're not sure, ask.

• *Constantly evaluate.* I spend a few minutes on my computer after every meeting. I even have a laptop computer and pocket tape recorder that I take to retreats and camps to keep a running diary. Simple notations about how the events or activities went—strengths, weaknesses, and suggestions for the future—all help. It is a good backup for any later questions. Try to answer questions before they come up. As a pastor, I do this with my sermons and worship services. I place my sermon notes in a small, brown envelope, along with a copy of the church bulletin and notes on what went especially well. I also jot down suggestions for improvement and enclose that as well.

3. Develop your mission statement. "Have you ever wondered why a pigeon walks so funny? According to an interesting article in the Detroit Free Press, a pigeon walks the way it does so it can see where it's going. Since a pigeon can't adjust its focus as it moves, it actually has to bring its head to a complete stop between steps in order to refocus."[2] In our ministry with senior adults, we need to learn some lessons from the pigeons.

We need to refocus on where we are in relation to the world and the will of God and where we hope to be in our senior adult ministry.

Sometimes we have the same problem as the pigeon: We have a hard time seeing while we're moving. We also need to stop between steps. We need to refocus on where we are in relation to the world and the will of God and where we hope to be in our senior adult ministry. This isn't to say that we have to stop and pray about every little decision we make in ministry. However, we do need to know where we're going so that we can determine a specific way to get there.

Whether building or strengthening a seniors' ministry, you'll need to create a vision statement. Any basic vision statement of senior adult ministry should address the needs of seniors and their relationship to Christ. As you develop your vision statement, consider the seniors' basic needs: love; acceptance; security; varied and meaningful activities in learning; choices that are realistic; and consistent, quality time together. A vision statement outlines the key objectives of the senior adult ministry.

Nehemiah was a person of vision. We can learn much about a vision statement by reading about Nehemiah's leadership style. Proverbs 29:18 says, "Where there is no revelation, the people cast off restraint; but blessed is he who keeps the law." Where there is no vision, the people perish.

One person said that vision is "foresight with insight based on hindsight." Another said that vision is "seeing the invisible and making it visible." While yet another says, "Vision is an informed bridge from the present to the future." George Barna defined it like this: "Vision for ministry is a clear mental image of a preferable future imparted by God to His chosen servants and is based upon an accurate understanding of God, self and circumstances."[3]

We are leaders who provide vision. Nehemiah spent much time in preparation, and he encountered insurmountable problems. But he kept on.

I have found that a vision statement needs to be simple and clear. Our church is a senior adult church. We have no children, youth, or young adult programs. We specialize in ministering to senior adults. Our church name is "Palm West Community Church," so we have an acronym that is PWCC: Palm West Community Church—People Who Care Church.

Our basic vision at PWCC is to be people who care. This must permeate everything we do and every way we act. If you're building a new seniors' ministry, be sure it begins with the motive of caring for people. If you're strengthening your senior ministry program, evaluate how much your existing program focuses on caring. You may remember reading about the newly appointed pastor standing at the study window in the church, weeping while looking over the inner city's tragic conditions. A layperson sought to console the new pastor by saying, "Don't worry. After you've been here awhile, you'll get used to it." The young minister's reply, "Yes, I know. That's why I'm crying." It's imperative that we never lose sight of the ministry of caring when building or strengthening a senior adult group.

If you're building a new seniors' ministry, be sure it begins with the motive of caring for people.

Think of Jesus' prayer found in John 17. Jesus had two requests of God in that prayer. First was a request that his body, the church, be one—to unify (John 17:20-23). Jesus' second request in that prayer was that God would be glorified, or to glorify (John 17:24-26). Following that example, it's clear that Jesus desires his body (the church) to come together as a family; to unify; and, through that unity, to glorify and praise God.

I caution that you not get hung up on nitpicking the differences between certain words. Words such as *purpose, mission, vision,* and *motto* can bog you down. Rather, take time to reflect on who you are and what you and your group really want to accomplish. Jot that down, decide how you can accomplish it, and get to work. One basic principle that I learned many years ago is "Do not major on the minor." Plan your work, and work your plan. It's too easy to lose focus and get detoured. Remember one of Murphy's laws: If you have enough meetings over a long enough period of time, the meetings become more important than the problem the meetings were intended to solve. Develop your mission statement, but keep it simple.

4. Set goals and objectives. Brainstorm the necessary goals and objectives to fulfill your mission statement. Objectives will be unique to fit your own situation. They also need to be achievable, measurable, understandable, specific, and realistic. Prioritize each objective for your senior adult ministry.

Goals and objectives are important to maintain focus. Remember the pigeons and how they focus? Because it cannot adjust its focus as it moves, the pigeon actually has to bring its head to a complete stop between steps in order to refocus. That is exactly what we must do. Set goals and objectives, then keep check on whether they're being reached. It's important for the pastor to have goals and to lead the congregation in setting goals. It is important to have long-term goals as well as short-term goals. It's also important to have spiritual, physical, emotional, social, and numerical goals. For example, my personal goals for one year answered several key questions that I wrote out:

- How many seniors would I like to see involved in shepherd groups, Sunday morning Bible studies, Sunday evening services, Wednesday evening prayer group, and/or midweek morning Bible study groups? After prayerful consideration and reflection, I jotted down what I thought was a realistic number for that coming year.
- How many seniors would I like to see involved in a daily Bible reading program, *either* reading through the Bible in one year, reading sermon texts in advance, or reading a devotional guide? After prayerful

consideration and reflection, I jotted down what I thought was a re-alistic number for the coming year.

- How many seniors would I like to see identify their spiritual gifts and find places of service in our church? Again I jotted down a number.
- How many seniors would I like to see make commitments to Christ and/or church membership? For this question, I jotted down a num-ber for each of the coming five years. I realized this was only a gen-eral guess or hope, but it gave me something to shoot for. In our case, we had just celebrated our fifth anniversary, so I was looking at where I thought we could be at our tenth anniversary.
- What will be our mission gifts for the coming years? Reflecting on what we had been able to do, I projected what I thought our seniors might be able to do if they stretched their faith. In our denomination we have four specific offerings during the year, so I jotted down what I felt we could do to increase each of these four offerings.
- What kind of training can we offer, and how often shall we offer it? Seniors love friendships, so I jotted down "Friendship Evangelism Training."
- Can we offer a yearly missions conference? I jotted down names of specific, nationally known speakers and possible dates for conferences for the upcoming years.
- Shall we schedule a Bible conference? Determine if your seniors would like to have a guest speaker, either local or nationally known, to lead a Bible conference weekend or retreat.
- Shall we establish short-term fellowship groups? This might include small group lunches or dinners in homes or local restaurants.
- Do we want to have a monthly luncheon at the church or a local restaurant or regularly scheduled social events? If so, how often and what types?
- How can we reach new residents in our area (seniors reaching seniors)?
- What should be our attendance goals for the coming several years?
- What long-term goals can we set?

You'll notice that this list of goals began with a spiritual focus and ended with numerical or financial goals.

It's important that the congregation or seniors' group is involved in goal-setting as well. For this reason it's good to have a planning day when everyone has the opportunity to give input. Begin with brainstorming at the start, followed by establishing ideas that help bring focus. We have a yearly planning day in January when our newly elected leaders begin their term of office. Again, it's important that there be consensus building, teamwork, and focus. At the end of the planning time, everyone should leave with a clear understanding of the goals that have been set.

5. Dream big, but live in reality. Look at your potential or existing senior adult ministry through growth eyes. Dream and catch a vision. Remember that dreaming big while living in reality does not necessarily mean thinking in terms of numbers. I personally feel that in Christian circles we tend to go from fad to fad, losing sight of the big picture. I remember well the days when almost every book in every Christian bookstore was on Bible prophecy. After that it changed to biblical authority, arguing about definitions of key words. The Holy Spirit and Charismatic movements came next. And of course, there had to be a time of fussing about what style of worship and what types of music were "right or wrong." In recent days we read about "Worship Wars," which seems to me to be a total contradiction of terms.

> **Remember that dreaming big while living in reality does not necessarily mean thinking in terms of numbers.**

To dream big and live in reality means that we understand God's call to ministry for our own lives and the lives of those we are trying to lead. Senior adults have all lived a long time. They have been in churches for many years. For the most part, I have found them to be tired of fighting church battles and bureaucracy.

Seniors are looking for love, acceptance, affirmation, fulfillment, encouragement, and practical help for their daily lives. It's important to learn that the success or failure of a senior adult ministry depends on your ability to refashion your dreams to fit reality. Some dreams may be accomplished right away. Some may take a year or two. Some may never be accomplished.

I was twelve years old when our family moved from Illinois to California. We began attending a very small church. I would guess they had about forty to fifty people in worship each Sunday morning. But the size of the congregation had nothing to do with the impact on lives. The pastor of that small congregation began to disciple me. He asked me to read Scripture in evening service. He took me out with him visiting homes of members and friends. I watched him, and I learned about ministry. That pastor had a dream of discipling others. Some thought that congregation was relatively insignificant because of its small size. But in looking back, I know of many from that small fellowship who went into Christian ministry, and each has impacted scores of others. In God's eyes, there are no "small" churches. It is important that we dream big but live in reality. You will have to modify your dreams. It will take time and patience.

9 SPECIFICS TO BUILD A SENIOR ADULT MINISTRY

You may want to refer to the ministry tool handout on page 57 as you work through these nine specifics.

1. Plan your program. How will each objective be accomplished? Who will be responsible for what? What supplies are needed? Who will supply what? With whom do you need to coordinate? What is the timeline? Establish a completion date for each detail of preparation. Begin small and build. Build one program and ministry at a time. Follow these three guidelines as you move ahead:

- *Quality produces quantity.* It's important to run an excellent ministry for seniors, no matter how small it is at first.
- *Quantity makes possible even more quality.* As your senior ministry grows, you will be able to accomplish more. With a larger group, you can bring in nationally known singers, speakers, and special guests.

An even higher quality ministry is possible with larger numbers if the leaders are careful to maintain quality.

- *Quantity that does not include the highest quality will be counterproductive!* If you seek numbers only and cannot maintain the highest standard of excellence, your ministry will diminish.[4]

A seniors' ministry needs to be built on quality that produces quantity. Years ago I planned a vacation Bible school. The recruitment and training was perfect. That summer I was also being ordained. I invited a former professor to be the speaker. He arrived a few days early, and I was proudly showing him the magnificent job I had done. As we stood outside the church, I announced that he was about to see something truly amazing. At that moment a bell rang and every door in the education building opened. Perfectly straight lines of leaders and children went from one room to the other, and then all doors closed. My face was beaming in eager anticipation of his response. His statement: "Wonderful organization, but do they know that you love them?"

A seniors' ministry needs to be built on quality that produces quantity.

Your relationship with your seniors is critical in building your senior adult ministry. Communication is all-important. I have found it effective to "over-communicate." Keep every senior adult in your ministry informed. Provide copies of schedules and information. The church secretary must know details in order to answer questions. Keeping everyone informed heads off the "nobody told me" conflicts prevalent in senior adult ministry.

Coordinate with key people. A music minister may have planned a musical that requires extra rehearsal times. The youth pastor may want a special event to welcome children graduating into the youth program. You need to know what other people have planned to avoid scheduling conflicts, and vice versa.

Communicate simply and clearly. When you differ with someone, do not argue, interrupt, jump to conclusions, or pass judgment. Do not assume that your understanding is the same as the other person's until you investigate. Try to hear what the other person is saying and ask helpful questions.

Use "I" messages and reflective listening. "I" messages tell the other person how you feel. A simple formula for an "I" message is "When you [the other person's actions], I feel [your feeling]." "I" messages put your feelings into nonconfrontational words.

Demonstrate reflective listening by saying, "What I understand you are saying is that you are feeling [your understanding of the other person's feelings] because [your understanding of the reason]." Ask if that is an accurate understanding. Show interest and express empathy. Be silent when silence is needed.

2. Choose your curriculum. In choosing a good curriculum, ensure sound biblical teaching combined with creative interaction of learners. If the curriculum has the teacher talking the entire time, avoid it. And the subject matter should be relevant to senior adult lives.

3. Set up your schedule. Ask yourself: When will each event occur? Will it conflict with other programs? Where will the event take place? Is the location suited for seniors? What coordination is necessary? What planning and publicity is required? Place dates on the master church calendar to guard against over-scheduling and scheduling conflicts.

4. Recruit staff. Simply listing personnel needs and asking for volunteers from the pulpit may produce no response or may produce volunteers who lack qualifications and suitability. It would be just as effective to run down the aisle on Sunday morning, grab "just anyone" amid protest, and hurry him or her off to a senior adult class to teach. Here are helpful steps in the recruitment process:

- Develop clearly written job descriptions, and prayerfully search for people to match those needs.
- Present the challenge, and give time for the potential volunteers to observe the ministry in action.

- Allow adequate time for people to seek God's leading.
- Finally, ask for a decision, and provide pre-service and ongoing in-service training. If the important ministries of senior adults in the church are to be Christ-honoring and life-molding, you must take care to discover, motivate, recruit, and train workers.

---

5. Arrange transportation. Begin with individuals in the church who can help provide transportation for those in need. As the need increases, rent a small wheelchair-accessible van or even charter a bus for special events. Do not go anywhere without an "emergency form" (sample on p. 108) giving necessary information about insurance on each senior, relatives to contact in an emergency, and medications they take or may need.

6. Prepare your facilities. Start with what you have, even if you have only one small room. Clean the room, and make the bulletin boards look attractive. Take pictures at all events, and have unique photos enlarged as posters to decorate the walls. The classroom can be used as a social room as well.

7. Coordinate publicity. Take pictures at all events. Send postcards and fliers often. And of course, encourage word-of-mouth. Take advantage of every opportunity to publicize. Local newspapers, public service announcements on local radio stations, information boards at retirement centers, and supermarkets may all give free publicity for your senior adult ministry.

> Remember that today's traditions were once someone's dreams. Today's dreams may become tomorrow's traditions.

8. Establish a budget. What supplies and materials do you need, and where will they come from? Where will the money come from? If you have a church board or congregation trapped by a fear of spending, be patient. Change takes time. Remember that today's traditions were once someone's dreams. Today's dreams may become tomorrow's traditions. Simply because committee or board members have never spent money on what you are proposing is a poor reason to turn down your proposal.

9. Evaluate. Continuously evaluate every program. Have regular meetings to evaluate. Use a prayer/suggestion box so that folks can contribute their ideas anonymously. This gives input in two ways: First, by their very presence! Giving input and being involved encourages their presence. Second, people feel free to write anonymously what they really feel. This becomes a nonthreatening way of evaluating everything. Find out what your senior adults like and do not like, then eliminate the things they do not enjoy. People change, so keep asking questions. Listen to your seniors and really get to know them. Constantly look for ways to improve your senior adult ministry.

A BIBLICAL VIEW OF AGING

Read the following Scripture references to discover how the Bible addresses aging and longevity. The Bible reference is given in column one. In column two, briefly jot down what the verse says about aging or longevity. In column three note your own personal response:

Bible Reference	What the Bible Verse Says About Aging	My Response
Ecclesiastes 3:1-2		
Genesis 1:27		
1 Kings 3:14		
Proverbs 10:27		
Job 12:12		
Deuteronomy 32:7		
Psalm 71:18		
Psalm 92:14		
Psalm 1:3		
Isaiah 46:4		
Psalm 71:9		
Leviticus 19:32		
1 Timothy 5:1-2		
Isaiah 65:22		
1 Corinthians 15:58		
Galatians 5:22-23		
2 Peter 3:18		

THE NEEDS OF SENIOR ADULTS IN THE 21ST CENTURY

For three minutes brainstorm why you feel there would be a need for senior adult ministry today.

Share your insights with others, and compile your list of ideas here:

List some benefits of starting or strengthening a senior adult ministry in your church.

Compile your list of ideas here, then share your insights with others on your ministry team.

---

5 THINGS TO CONSIDER BEFORE STARTING A SENIOR ADULT MINISTRY

Beginning on page 39 of Chapter 2, there was a discussion of what to do before beginning a new senior adult ministry. Jot down any insights gleaned from the following five points:

1. Prayer:

2. Counting the cost:

3. Developing a mission statement:

4. Setting goals and objectives:

5. Dreaming big, but living in reality:

DEALING WITH CONFLICT

Thinking of conflict in the church, particularly in senior adult ministry, five basic approaches were given:

- Surrender

- Subversion

- Open warfare

- Adjustment

- Negotiation

As you think of your ministry, particularly your senior adults...

1. Which of the five approaches have you seen "in action"?

2. How serious were the consequences that resulted?

3. What approaches to conflict resolution have provided positive results in your senior adult ministry?

4. Which seems to speak to you personally as something you can use directly in your ministry?

9 SPECIFICS TO BUILD A SENIOR ADULT MINISTRY

Of the nine specific steps to strengthen your senior adult ministry, which are you already doing, and which should you begin? Fill in the chart below:

Step	Accomplished	Steps To Take	Date For Completion
Plan your program:			
Choose your curriculum:			
Set up your schedule:			
Recruit staff:			
Arrange transportation:			
Prepare your facilities:			
Coordinate publicity:			
Establish a budget:			
Evaluate:			

RESPONSE QUESTIONS

1. How much weekly prayer time do I spend for my senior adult ministry? Is that enough?

2. Have I shared my dreams and vision for seniors with lay people in my church? List the names of people with whom you've shared your vision, the names of your prayer support group, and where and when you meet or plan to meet.

3. Do I have a clear mission statement for the senior adult ministry?

4. What are my objectives for the coming months? for the next five years?

5. What existing ministries do we have for senior adults in our church right now?

6. Which of these programs is most effective? least effective?

7. What can be done to improve the ineffective program, or should it be cut?

8. What are some new senior adult activities, events, programs, or ministries that I would like to implement in the next year?

9. How would I rate our current senior adult curriculum?

10. Who are potential volunteers that could observe and be trained in our senior adult ministry?

11. How can others be involved in transportation and evaluation?

12. How can our outreach for senior adults be expanded in our area?

13. How can our facilities be improved for seniors? our publicity?

14. How can our current senior ministry budget be better utilized?

15. How can others be involved in more meaningful ways?

CHAPTER 3

INVOLVING SENIOR ADULTS IN MINISTRY

It has been said, and perhaps it's true, that life begins at fifty but everything else starts to wear out, fall out, or spread out. It's a myth that senior adults no longer want to contribute. It's equally untrue that senior adults don't want to be actively involved. Senior adults *do* want to be involved. In this chapter we'll look at ways you can directly involve seniors in ministry.

It's a myth that senior adults no longer want to contribute. It's equally untrue that senior adults don't want to be actively involved. Senior adults *do* want to be involved.

7 MUSTS FOR INVOLVING SENIOR ADULTS

There are numerous creative ways to involve senior adults in the church, but following are seven basic musts to get you started.

1. Cultivate a congregation that is fellowship-oriented and caring in nature. One way to cultivate a fellowship-oriented and caring congregation is with care or shepherd groups. Many churches have found that small groups help create this warmth and caring fellowship. The following simple principles can serve as helpful guidelines in creating small care or shepherd groups in your senior adult ministry.

- *Find one specific individual to be responsible.* One person must know how to delegate. He or she forms a task force or committee to assist. While the senior pastor should be aware of the importance of small care groups and should enthusiastically share that vision with the congregation, ultimately one specific person must be responsible for overseeing the shepherd group ministry for senior adults.

- *Know who you want to reach.* There will be varied needs within the senior adult group. Some will be interested in an in-depth Bible study. Others will desire more informal social fellowship times that include games and light conversation. Still others will be looking for a more in-depth personal sharing of struggles, such as times in life when they have experienced loss. You must know whom you desire to reach in order to create shepherd groups that will truly meet needs.

- *Set up a plan.* After you carefully and prayerfully consider the need for shepherd groups, then you'll need to plan. It may be wise to begin at a time when most seniors are already actively involved. For example, summer tends to not be a good time to initiate a group because many senior adults leave for extended trips. The fall, when people are returning home, might be a better time to begin. Use surveys, church newsletters, posters, and fliers to help communicate information about the shepherd groups that will be starting up.

If you begin shepherd groups without careful preparation, good leadership, and a clear purpose, the groups probably will not succeed. It's better to proceed slowly, prayerfully, and methodically.

- *Have a simple, clear purpose for the shepherd groups.* A good beginning is imperative. If you begin shepherd groups without careful preparation, good leadership, and a clear purpose, the groups probably will not succeed. It's better to proceed slowly, prayerfully, and methodically. You'll also want to constantly remind the group of the need for shepherd groups.

- *Communicate exactly what you are offering.* To determine who is interested in shepherd groups, it may be helpful to use an all-church survey (see sample survey on page 74 at the end of this chapter). Make your plans according to the survey results, then clearly communicate your plans. Senior adults will not continue to be involved in activities they feel are not worth their time or energy. Let your seniors know that these groups are not only for members and regular attendees, but are also a wonderful means for outreach. Those attending a group may invite a friend or neighbor to join them. The groups can become a powerful outreach tool.

After tabulating the information received from the survey, begin the process of organizing the various shepherd groups that meet the needs of your seniors. You may have groups dealing with family issues or general interests. Some groups may center on addictions, compulsions, or relational problems. Loss and trauma issues are also important among many seniors. Every group must be centered on the love of Jesus, and every group should meet regularly. While confidentiality within the group is important, it will be necessary to ensure that the group does not become thought of as some "secret" group.

Shepherd groups should be places where people can come together for healing and release, where God can work in their lives. Some seniors will come in brokenness, looking for healing. Others may come looking for simple encouragement and socialization. Shepherd groups provide the opportunity to involve people and bring vitality and growth to your senior adult ministry and, ultimately, to the entire congregation. Be sure your groups emphasize involvement, fellowship, acceptance, and caring.

2. Involve everyone in some way. There is an old adage, "Use me or lose me." This is especially true with senior adults. There's a prayer that says, "I am only one, but I am one; I cannot do everything, but I can do something. What I can do, I ought to do, and what I ought to do, by God's grace I will do."[1]

Many hands lighten the workload. In the Bible, Moses had a problem when the people lined up to bring their concerns to him. Moses' father-in-law, Jethro, gave him the wonderful solution: delegation. Exodus 18:13-27 says, "The next day Moses took his seat to serve as judge for the people, and they stood around him from morning till evening. When his father-in-law saw all that Moses was doing for the people, he said, 'What is this you are doing for the people? Why do you alone sit as judge, while all these people stand around you from morning till evening?'

Moses answered him, 'Because the people come to me to seek God's will. Whenever they have a dispute, it is brought to me, and I decide between the parties and inform them of God's decrees and laws.'

"Moses' father-in-law replied, 'What you are doing is not good. You and these people who come to you will only wear yourselves out. The work is too heavy for you; you cannot handle it alone. Listen now to me and I will give you some advice, and may God be with you. You must be the people's representative before God and bring their disputes to him. Teach them the decrees and laws, and show them the way to live and the duties they are to perform. But select capable men from all the people—men who fear God, trustworthy men who hate dishonest gain—and appoint them as officials over thousands, hundreds, fifties and tens. Have them serve as judges for the people at all times, but have them bring every difficult case to you; the simple cases they can decide themselves. That will make your load lighter, because they will share it with you. If you do this and God so commands, you will be able to stand the strain, and all these people will go home satisfied.'

> "I am only one, but I am one; I cannot do everything, but I can do something. What I can do, I ought to do, and what I ought to do, by God's grace I will do."

"Moses listened to his father-in-law and did everything he said. He chose capable men from all Israel and made them leaders of the people, officials over thousands, hundreds, fifties and tens. They served as judges for the people at all times. The difficult cases they brought to Moses, but the simple ones they decided themselves. Then Moses sent his father-in-law on his way, and Jethro returned to his own country."

We, too, need to practice the art of delegation by involving others as much as we can.

3. Lead by example. The standards, commitment, and quality of leadership will never rise above the standards, commitment, and quality of the person that is at the top. As a leader in senior adult ministry, you are a pacesetter. Your example is crucial. Your standards, your commitment, and your quality of leadership will be powerful examples to those in your ministry. The longer you minister in a particular group, the more important these qualities become. A strong, Christlike senior adult leader is one who walks ahead of the group without being detached from the group. This leader influences those in the group and moves them toward specific goals.

I have found that strong leaders in senior adult groups are those who are authentic. They realize the awesome responsibility that is theirs. They understand the overall picture of where the church is going, and they help align the senior adult ministry with that broader vision. Effective senior adult leaders not only listen well, they also know how to respond to differences and even to harsh criticism. They can sense the pulse of the group and earn respect over time.

Strong leaders lead with clear thinking, not emotions. They follow through on details. Most of all, strong leaders are people of prayer.

Strong leaders lead with clear thinking, not emotions. They follow through on details. Most of all, strong leaders are people of prayer.

4. Meet the specific needs of senior adults. Senior adults are spiritually hungry. Hungry people need to be fed. Senior adults who are spiritually hungry are looking for a group that provides not only social fellowship, which is important, but one that will also meet spiritual needs. There's no limit to the number of seniors a church can reach if it provides sound biblical teaching with a balanced ministry of love and care.

5. Evaluate growth by spiritual and emotional health, not just by numbers or financial growth. For too many years the church has equated success with numerical growth. The numbers game can cause us to lose focus. Many years ago, I learned that numbers change quickly. Yes, it's important to see numerical growth, but only if the numbers represent individuals and their needs. Numbers must always be the byproduct of needs that have been met. To become myopic and focus on numbers alone brings frustration, discouragement, and defeat.

It's more realistic to watch for trends and look at the bigger picture. There are always reasons for attendance changes, either up or down. One group may constantly bring in special musical groups and other attractions, which builds attendance quickly. Another group may have a dynamic personality working with its senior adults. What's truly important is being faithful to God's calling. We must evaluate growth by the spiritual and emotional health of our seniors, not just by numerical or financial growth.

6. Encourage continuing usefulness among senior adults in the congregation. For too long we've given the impression that when someone reaches a certain age, he or she is no longer effective in ministry. More often, just the opposite is true. Many senior adults have a wealth of experience and are highly effective workers. Our job is to encourage continued usefulness among our senior adults. There comes a time when seniors are no longer able to effectively continue their active involvement. However, even then they can successfully serve in less active roles. For example, most older adults can be involved in meaningful ministry through "telecare" ministry (follow-up of people by use of the telephone) and prayer. We must encourage the continuing usefulness of all of our senior adults.

> **We must encourage the continuing usefulness of all of our senior adults.**

7. Laugh with those who laugh, and cry with those who cry. Humor is a golden key for all ages, but especially for senior adults. Sensitivity is crucial. Know when to laugh, when to be silent, and when to cry with senior adults. Laughter and good, positive humor are wonderful medicine for hurting hearts. Proverbs 17:22 reminds us that "a cheerful heart is good medicine, but a crushed spirit dries up the bones."

50 PRACTICAL WAYS TO INVOLVE SENIOR ADULTS IN MINISTRY

Involve your senior adults by...

1. setting up a seniors' group e-mail prayer chain. (Sample Prayer Card included as a ministry tool page at the end of this chapter.)

2. establishing a "telecare" ministry. (More on this in Chapter 4 under

"5 Golden Keys to Reaching Out to Seniors.")

3. acquiring a telephone answering machine, voice mail, or answering service. Have the phone company install a separate line, and use that number as an information center or hot line. Seniors can call anytime to get details for upcoming events, activities, and/or prayer requests.

4. having senior adults reflect on insights they have gained after each study, small group, or meeting. Have seniors write down notes or discuss these insights in small groups.

5. having senior adults put together a "Seniors Yearbook" at the end of the year. It should include photos and articles about the past year's activities. It will remind them of the good times they shared and bring joy to their lives.

6. having senior adults set up a "phone chain" to help spread the word regarding upcoming events. If you have ten people who will call ten others, you can contact a hundred people in one evening. Personal contact is always effective.

7. having senior adults select their leadership. It's easier to enlist those leaders when the group has chosen them.

8. having senior adults meet regularly with your volunteer staff for training, for prayer, and for fellowship.

9. having senior adults host local international students at a dinner in their honor. Have the students tell about being in their country and how that differs from the United States. Present each one with a gift certificate for a free call home. If possible, have students stay overnight with one of your seniors.

10. having senior adults plan some early-morning activities. There will be few schedule conflicts, and they will enjoy the adventure. Most seniors are early risers. Avoid planning events on days that conflict with community events.

11. having senior adults get together to go out to breakfast or lunch just to visit; no agendas.

12. having senior adults select times that are the best for the members of the group. Remember that mornings are normally great and evenings are normally out.

13. getting to know the families of your seniors. Get acquainted with their children, grandchildren, and great-grandchildren.

14. having senior adults wear name tags. Encourage your seniors to wear name tags at all events.

15. having senior adults find positive ways for their group to become involved in the life of the church, not just the life of their group. Encourage senior adults to serve on boards and committees, working with children or participating in worship and attending other events and meetings.

16. having senior adults visit people in their homes. They should always call to set up an appointment first.

17. having senior adults print up a brochure or postcard that describes their group and its activities. They could include photos, brief descriptions, times, and locations (if known) and make these brochures available to everyone.

18. having senior adults plan at least one retreat each year. One day at a retreat is worth a month of Sundays.

19. having senior adults take a Red Cross first-aid course. Encourage others on your staff to do the same. Encourage senior adults to know CPR, and have emergency procedures in place.

20. having senior adults offer to serve as volunteer chaplains at a local hospital or hospice unit or drug and alcohol treatment program.

21. having senior adults prepare a "Most Unusual Hat" contest. Ask people to come with ridiculous-looking hats, and then hold a contest to determine first-, second-, and third-place winners.

22. sending thank you notes.

23. having senior adults prepare an intergenerational meeting with children, youth, and young adult groups.

24. putting up audiovisual equipment, such as an overhead projector. If songs are copyrighted, get permission before displaying the lyrics.

25. having senior adults keep people informed. Have them publish a newsletter or schedule periodic meetings for questions and to provide input. Lack of communication can seriously handicap your ministry.

26. having senior adults get a resource directory from your denomination. It will save you hours when you want to find the best resource for any situation.

27. having senior adults set a goal for each activity and see if the goal is met. This will give you direction for everything you do.

28. developing good job descriptions for your volunteer leaders. Make sure they know exactly what's expected of senior adults, as well as what is *not* expected of senior adults. Provide senior adults with good resources for the jobs you've asked them to do.

29. conducting brainstorming sessions with your group to foster creativity. Allow ideas to flow without criticism. Evaluate only after the ideas have stopped.

30. having senior adults share their special concerns or needs (such as a personality, emotional, physical, or spiritual problem). Never assume that they are already being helped.

31. having senior adults check out the curriculum and resources. Adapt it to the needs of your own senior group. Curriculum writers do not know your seniors; you do.

32. having senior adults prepare a place to keep clip art, brochures, cartoons, drawings, illustrations, and lettering that you find from time to time. These can be used later for designing your own publications and announcements.

33. having senior adults keep accurate attendance records. Do not worry about numerical growth. Size does not equal success. Health leads to growth, not vice versa. Encourage them to send "missed you" cards when people are absent.

34. having senior adults prepare a personal bulletin board or Web site where they post pictures of family and friends, seniors, classic postcards, and other things that you collect.

35. having senior adults confirm any group reservations or bus charters the day before the event.

36. having senior adults prepare refreshments for meetings and activities. It's a relatively easy thing to do, and senior adults love food. It also encourages people to stay and socialize, allowing for personal interaction.

37. having senior adults obtain free films and videotapes that are available from the local public library.

38. keeping a picture of each person in a photo book. Get family and personal information, vital statistics, photos, notes from personal interviews and observations, and other information. Keep it confidential. Not only will it benefit your ministry, but it also will make a wonderful gift for your successor.

39. having senior adults plan and prepare a retreat to provide an opportunity for planning and team building.

40. having senior adults play musical instruments. This will build their confidence and leadership ability.

41. having senior adults volunteer to read or answer a question. Never call on someone without asking in advance.

42. having senior adults check out camps and conferences. Never believe conference center brochures. Always have someone visit a facility before booking. Ask questions about flexibility, additional costs, and availability of "extras." Eat a meal there if possible, and be sure to check on whether the facility is wheelchair-accessible.

43. having senior adults use television to tape and discuss good programs. Discuss and evaluate the programs that are most interesting to your seniors.

44. having senior adults provide coffee and donuts, a salad bar, or some other refreshment after the worship service as a gift to the church.

45. having senior adults involved in at least one service project each year. Service projects not only give people a chance to make a positive contribution to someone's life, but they also are great for building community.

46. having senior adults put on a drama once a year. This gives more people a chance to use their talents and be in the limelight.

47. having senior adults prepare job descriptions for each role within the ministry.

48. having senior adults prepare and lead a mission project.

49. having senior adults develop programs that reflect the needs, interests, and energy level of senior adults.

50. having senior adults prepare an overnight or weekend trip for senior adults.

DEALING WITH CRITICISM IN SENIOR ADULT MINISTRY

As you involve seniors in ministry, you will most likely experience criticism. They'll criticize one another, and they'll criticize you. The real goal of a shared senior adult ministry is to help seniors get beyond criticism and instead build consensus despite their differences (see the Consensus Building Do's and Don'ts ministry tool on page 75). When criticism comes, there are two basic and simple concepts that will help you respond instead of react.

The real goal of a shared senior adult ministry is to help seniors get beyond criticism and instead build consensus despite their differences.

First, if you're criticized for something you've said or done, see if there is any truth in the criticism. If you find that in fact you are or were in the wrong, accept the criticism graciously and ask for forgiveness. "If you're in the wrong, you don't have a defense."[1] Attempting to rationalize or defend yourself will only be counterproductive, and you'll quickly lose your self-respect, as well as the respect of your senior groups. You should respond with, "You're right; I was wrong."

Second, if you believe you're right, you don't need to defend yourself.[2] Defending yourself only creates more problems and prolongs the situation. Prolonging the situation allows the hurt and fractured relationship to grow in its unhealthy state. The healthy thing to do is just move on. Fill out the "Dealing With Criticism Questionnaire" on page 76 to further prepare yourself for handling critical remarks.

You should also understand how seniors react to criticism. When senior adults are criticized or rejected they often respond by…

- *gossip or retaliation.* Some people defend against rejection by seeking acceptance through control, competition, and performance. Gossiping and undermining others are natural reactions. Help your senior adults learn how to respond rather than react.
- *outwardly agreeing or giving in.* The majority of people today defend

The majority of people today defend against rejection by simply giving in or agreeing in order to gain approval and acceptance.

against rejection by simply giving in or agreeing in order to gain approval and acceptance. Deep down inside, however, they probably resent the criticism and may retaliate in passive ways.

• *rebellion.* They'll say, "I don't need you or this church." Misplaced anger can be highly destructive.

• *defensiveness.* They may defend their actions, even if they know they're wrong.

All of these reactions only prolong the conflict. We need to teach seniors how to handle criticism in a way that fosters healing and resolution, not hurt and anger.

When dealing with criticism yourself, here are some questions you can ask to help you deal with it in a healthy way:

1. What events, rejections, or criticisms in my past might be possible sources of bitterness for me today?

2. What motivates me to want to struggle to forgive the person who criticized or rejected me?

3. What might give me the courage to face past rejections, criticisms, or hurts?

4. What would I like to say to God about past criticisms, rejections, or hurts that I have experienced?

5. What do I usually do when I am rejected or criticized by someone who is very important to me?

6. What are my thoughts and feelings about myself when I am criticized or rejected?

7. How can other people be helpful to me in my struggle with dealing with rejection and criticism?

8. Why is it so difficult to forgive those who have hurt me?

9. What criticism, rejection, or hurtful experience would I like to be able to give to God? What makes it difficult to do so?

10. Why is it difficult for me to let go of criticism? What will it take for me to let go of it? When will I let this go?

Seniors have so much to offer if we'll just be willing to release them into ministry. We are no longer in the days of ministry simply *to* seniors. A true senior adult ministry in the twenty-first century will be a ministry not only *to* seniors but also *of* seniors.

A true senior adult ministry in the twenty-first century will be a ministry not only *to* seniors but also *of* seniors.

ALL-CHURCH SURVEY

The following survey is designed to assist us in the development of shepherd groups. These groups have the potential for spiritual growth and acquiring new friends. Please take a few moments to check the following questions that fit your specific needs, desires, or interests.

I would...

be interested in a group of __ 4, __ 8, __ 12 members.
prefer a group consisting of __ all men, __ all women, __ couples, __ mixed.
prefer a group that meets __ once a week, __ bimonthly, __ monthly.
prefer a group that meets __ mornings, __ afternoons, __ evenings.
I am interested in __ year-round, __ winter months only.

The type of group I would enjoy would emphasize
(check all that apply):

__ variety of games and conversation

__ conversation focused on current events

__ willingness to learn how to be a leader

__ meeting located at the church

__ sharing personal growth and struggles

__ in-depth Bible study/prayer

__ reading and reviewing books

__ rotating location in each member's home

__ other: _____

__ My present activities prevent me from joining a group.

__ Would you be interested in joining a "breakfast group"? This group would meet at the church for a brief devotional (presented on a rotation basis by members of the group), prayer, and then would go to a local restaurant for breakfast.

__ men's breakfast group, __ women's breakfast group, __ mixed breakfast group

Name: _____ **Phone**: _____

CONSENSUS BUILDING: DO'S AND DON'TS

You have achieved consensus decisions when all members of your group support the decision, though it may not be exactly what each of them wants. Consensus decisions are better than decisions arrived at through voting or executive order because everyone supports them—they all "buy into" the decision. This makes implementation much easier. Here are some do's and don'ts for volunteer leaders working for consensus decisions:

Do	Don't
get all your assumptions and issues on the table.	come to easy, early agreements or compete or argue.
get everyone to participate, and do listen to everyone's input.	vote (though "straw votes" are OK).
look at disagreements as opportunities to get new points of view.	compete or argue strongly for extreme positions.
consider all the alternatives before jumping to a solution.	make "executive decisions" if you can avoid it.
decide the criteria for a good solution before discussing alternative solutions.	talk about solutions until everyone agrees on the problem.
use problem-solving techniques.	allow the group to attack one person's ideas.
get all the data you can on the issue.	be negative.
make sure all people to be affected by the decision help make the decision.	discourage divergent points of view.

DEALING WITH CRITICISM QUESTIONNAIRE

Complete the following statements by circling one of these words: always, usually, sometimes, rarely.

- I [always, usually, sometimes, rarely] know my limitations and respect senior adults.
- I'm [always, usually, sometimes, rarely] honest with others about how I feel.
- I [always, usually, sometimes, rarely] feel deep rejection when someone criticizes me.
- I [always, usually, sometimes, rarely] become quite defensive when I hear of someone criticizing my work or me.

People have different ways of dealing with criticism. When someone criticizes you or your work, what do you do typically?

❑ *What? Me get criticized?*
❑ *I blow up.*
❑ *I quietly count to ten inside my head.*
❑ *I yell a lot, but it's all just hot air.*
❑ *I deal directly with the source of the criticism in a constructive way.*
❑ *I hold my breath and turn purple.*
❑ *I take it out on my kids or dog.*
❑ *I do a slow burn.*

❑ *I just push it away and slap on a plastic smile.*
❑ *I assume I'm probably overreacting.*
❑ *I get cutting and sarcastic.*
❑ *I act like there is no problem.*
❑ *I sulk.*
❑ *I blame others.*
❑ *I make excuses.*
❑ *I go exercise and work off being upset.*

Your responses will determine whether the criticism and rejection you'll occasionally experience in your senior adult ministry will contribute to or deter you from your spiritual growth.

PRAYER CARD

Partners in Prayer

If you have a prayer request or update, fill in this card and place it in the offering plate.

Name: _____

Home Phone: _____ Work Phone: _____

E-mail: _____

Address: _____

City: _____ State: _____ ZIP: _____

If you would like more information on our prayer ministry, check the following box.

❏ Prayer Partner Ministry

Write prayer requests and updates on the other side.

Prayer Requests _____

_____

_____

_____

_____

Prayer Updates _____

_____

_____

_____

_____

CHAPTER 4

REACHING OUT TO SENIOR ADULTS

As I think of reaching out to seniors, I reflect on Matthew 9:35-38: "Jesus went through all the towns and villages, teaching in their synagogues, preaching the good news of the kingdom and healing every disease and sickness. When he saw the crowds, he had compassion on them, because they were harassed and helpless, like sheep without a shepherd. Then he said to his disciples, 'The harvest is plentiful but the workers are few. Ask the Lord of the harvest, therefore, to send out workers into his harvest field.' " A parallel passage is in Luke 19:41: "As he approached Jerusalem and saw the city, he wept over it." Jesus modeled three simple outreach steps that can be applied to our senior adult ministry:

- Jesus came near.
- Jesus saw.
- Jesus wept.

I can think of no clearer picture of reaching out to seniors today than those three principles. For us to have effective senior adult ministries, we'll need to come near; that is, we'll need to spend time in the lives of our seniors. We'll need to feel their hurts and pain. We'll need to visit them, pray with them, laugh with them, and cry with them. Only then will we have eyes

For us to have effective senior adult ministries, we'll need to come near; that is, we'll need to spend time in the lives of our seniors. We'll need to feel their hurts and pain. We'll need to visit them, pray with them, laugh with them, and cry with them.

to see—spiritual eyes that are open to the loneliness, depression, hurt, and frustration of today's seniors.

I can think of no greater age group for outreach ministry opportunity than senior adults. When I say "outreach," I am *not* talking about buttonholing people and preaching *at* them. Outreach isn't so much a call for a decision as it is a call to become a disciple or follower of Christ. Seniors have made thousands of decisions during their lifetimes. They're not looking so much for religion as they are seeking a relationship. Those who are blessed to work with senior adults have a marvelous opportunity to show mature adults how they can have a meaningful relationship with Jesus and how this relationship bonds them together as part of God's family.

Jesus himself always called others to become disciples. Jesus was not just concerned with decisions; Jesus was also concerned with discipleship.

The New Testament is filled with examples of discipleship, God's way of bringing people to life. Jesus himself always called others to become disciples. Jesus was not just concerned with decisions; Jesus was also concerned with discipleship.

In the Winter 2000 issue of Abstracts On Aging, there appear some startling statistics on today's seniors. Think about the following as you consider reaching out to senior adults in your community:

- "Since January 1, 1996, one Baby Boomer has turned 50 every 90 seconds!"
- "In 1989 21 percent of Americans were over the age of 55; by the year 2020 they will represent nearly one third of the total U.S. population."
- "Households headed by individuals over age 55 have twice as many assets as those headed by 35-55 year olds; those over 75 have twice as many as those under 40."
- "Though per capita income peaks before the age of 65, discretionary income peaks after the age of 65."
- "Although those over 55 comprise only a little more than 20 percent of the population currently, they control 40 percent of total discretionary income."

- "The percentage of college educated seniors is growing faster than the senior segment as a whole."
- "While not early adapters of new technologies, seniors are users once they are well-established: 74 percent of seniors have VCRs and 62 percent have cable television."
- "According to studies by Daniel Yankelovich, 71 percent of seniors believe 'the key to being retired is keeping busy;' and 27 percent 'have a strong need to keep up with the latest developments in technology.' "
- "In his book *The Mature Market*, Robert S. Menchin claims that more than 50 percent of seniors are interested in trying new technologies and products."[1]

All of these facts should help bring focus to our outreach strategies for senior adults in the local church. In working within a specialized senior adult ministry, I have found five priorities that have been highly effective.

5 Golden Keys to Reaching Out to Seniors

1. Make outreach a top priority. If you have no goals, you'll never know if you've reached them. Goals are simply what we reach for, something to help us keep focus. One year while I was pastor of a senior adult community church, I jotted down a number (a specific goal) of people that I thought I might reach in the coming year. I decided on fifty people. To achieve that goal, outreach was crucial.

Since this was a new church start and a small congregation, this goal seemed unattainable. As we moved through that year, I kept praying about the goal of receiving fifty new members into our fellowship by the end of the year. As the months slipped away, I had to make outreach a top priority in the minds and hearts of every member of our congregation. I placed a large bulletin board at the back of the sanctuary with the pictures of the few new members we had received early that year. I put new members' pictures in the church newsletter, along with a nice write-up about each new member. I asked questions from the pulpit, such as how many new members they thought we might receive that year. I offered inquirers' classes that were fresh and fun and challenged everyone in the congregation to get involved in bringing friends, neighbors, and family with them to worship.

Every visitor that came was immediately telephoned. A team of two would go visit first-time visitors with a coffee mug filled with candy kisses. This became humorous in that they were known as the "Muggers." My wife and I would follow up with another visit, and we found that visitors were returning. Word got out that our little church was a warm, caring, and friendly church.

By November we were seven short of our goal. I could hardly believe that God had sent so many new members to become a part of our church family. I remember mentioning at the close of worship one Sunday that we were only seven short of a goal that I had set almost a year ago. The next Sunday morning, two more came forward, and one gentleman whispered in my ear, "Now you are only five short of your goal, pastor." When I told that to the congregation, I was eager to see what the response would be.

By December we were only one short of the goal of fifty that I had set a year before. And, you guessed it, just before the close of that year, one more couple came forward for membership, making our final count of new members for that year fifty-one. What a joy!

I found that some of those attending worship were driving many miles past scores of other churches to attend ours. Why? Because they found meaningful opportunities in our church.

2. Provide meaningful outreach opportunities using new and different ways to involve volunteers. In today's busy society, you simply cannot do business as usual. In a church where I served, I found that some of those attending worship were driving many miles past scores of other churches to attend ours. Why? Because they found meaningful opportunities in our church. And meaningful opportunities must be made available for those serving in the outreach ministry. Simply knocking on doors is no longer effective. In fact, I lived in a community where nearly every home was blocked by a security gate. In that community it was futile to think you could go door to door. We had to find new and different ways to do outreach ministry.

We established a "telecare" ministry. Telecare ministry is a practical twenty-first-century outreach ministry. A retired pastor in our congregation was a specialist in pastoral counseling. He came to me one day, offering his services to establish a ministry whereby there could be immediate follow-up of any new or missing people. We simply jotted down the names of new or missing folks on a Telecare Ministry Calling Report (see ministry tool sample on pages 103-104 at the end of this chapter), gave the form to the retired pastor, and the job was done. He had a group of volunteers that he had trained to telephone people. He gave them some basic information on what to say and some helpful, practical guidelines for meeting counseling needs. Scores of telephone calls were made every week through this meaningful outreach opportunity.

3. Utilize effective ministries of love and caring. Learning how to be a caring congregation takes time. I mentioned that our church is called the "People Who Care Church." That's our theme. Nearly everything we do flows from that basic premise. Senior adults love to be with other friends; they love a warm, loving, and caring church family. The best outreach program is happy people telling others about the source of their satisfaction. There is simply no substitute for people who really are happy. I can think of nothing more detrimental to outreach than for people to be invited to a warm and loving congregation only to find that they have been misled.

The best outreach program is happy people telling others about the source of their satisfaction.

Utilize effective ministries of love and caring. Canned talks at the front door are one of the fastest ways to turn off people to the love of Christ. On the other hand, genuine warmth and caring is one of the fastest ways to bring people to the love of Christ.

In a study of 720 people to whom the gospel had been presented, some interesting results were found.

The people in this study were asked to classify the person that shared the gospel with them into one of three categories: "friend," "teacher," or "salesman." The respondents that had viewed the person who talked to them about a relationship with Jesus as a friend had a much higher rate of becoming Christians and being active in church. For those who perceived the person sharing Christ with them as a salesman, but who still had made an initial positive decision, they subsequently "dropped out" at a much higher rate. And finally, the least effective presenter, according to this study, was that of teacher.[2]

No one wants a salesperson pushing anything on him or her, but don't we all want a friend? We need to be a friend to those who need a friend. We need to be a friend to those who need a personal relationship with Christ. We also must stop pushing and manipulating and leave the results up to God.

There is little question that relationship building is vital in sharing our faith. Seniors must tell other seniors of the love they have for Christ, but they must do so in a loving and caring way.

Being a friend is the most influential means of bringing people to faith in Christ.

Again it can easily be seen that a friend is the most influential means of bringing people to faith, reaching out through love and caring.

> **A friend is the most influential means of bringing people to faith, reaching out through love and caring.**

4. Place the focus on spiritual maturity that is based on demonstrated attitude and action. Bible knowledge is important; but knowledge for knowledge's sake, without life application, is of little value. Scripture emphasizes over and over the importance of putting into practice what we've heard. The entire book of James is about walking what we're talking. As we minister to senior adults, it's important that we create ways for them to put into practice what they're learning. Our focus must be on helping create spiritual maturity in the life of the senior (Colossians 1:28). We must see a change in attitude and action. What we believe should determine how we act as believers.

5. Train leadership and provide structures that are flexible and consistent. Finding and training quality leadership is critical. For too many years, the church has been guilty of grabbing people in the hallway and pushing them into a senior adult class that is without a teacher. This process can destroy a senior adult ministry. Instead, we need a careful, prayerful process of recruiting and training volunteers that will provide lasting results. I have found some simple steps to recruitment that are helpful:

- Nurture a positive recruitment atmosphere. Pray together as a team, and ask God for workers. No endeavor in the church can be successful without prayer. Involve everyone concerned about the ministry. Inform them of specific needs in the senior adult group. Pray to the Lord of harvest that God will raise up the workers to serve.
- Promote the needs to the congregation. Provide both pre-service and in-service training so that volunteers know exactly what they are to do.
- Provide clearly written job descriptions. Provide starting and ending dates. Too often someone offers to serve, only to find himself or herself abandoned in the position for life.
- Search prayerfully and carefully for the volunteers you need. Take adequate time. Never rush or jump into finding a quick fix.
- Secure approval from the powers that be before you ask the person to serve. Be sure to go through the proper channels so you don't have to backpedal. Then, after receiving the proper go-ahead, ask the person to serve. Challenge the person concerning the responsibility before the Lord. Remind him or her of your constant support and prayer.
- After additional prayer, time, and reflection, ask for a decision. If he or she agrees to serve, be sure to provide adequate training and support.

---

8 OUTREACH IDEAS FOR SENIOR ADULT GROUPS

Here are some simple ideas to jump-start your outreach to seniors.

1. *New prospects*—There are many unchurched senior adults living in our communities. Even those who are involved in other churches have needs that may not be met. Those seniors will want to be involved in an active and growing senior adult ministry. New families moving into your area are a notable opportunity for outreach. Train your church members to keep a watchful eye for moving vans. Have senior adult literature available, and invite new residents to attend your group. Encourage church families to bring friends with them to worship. Then be sure to follow up with all visitors. Scan the church's membership list for names of seniors who may be invited to the senior activities.

2. *Service organizations*—Many of your members volunteer in various service organizations in the community. Have them take senior adult ministry literature to their organizations for distribution.

3. *Community locations*—The public library is another good place to distribute senior adult ministry brochures. You could also try city libraries, Christian bookstores, social service organizations, community colleges, and local hospitals.

> **Children have grandparents, and grandparents are who you're looking for!**

4. *Your own church ministry*—Look over the names of those involved in the ministries of your church. See if you can find seniors who you could invite to the group. The church's children's ministries are especially good places to find potential seniors to involve in your ministry. Children have grandparents, and grandparents are who you're looking for! Also, don't overlook men's ministries, women's ministries, and choirs. Special ministries—such as vacation Bible school, special family events, and Christmas and Easter events—can provide names of seniors as well.

5. *Circles of influence*—Another basic starting place is each person's own personal circle of friends. Invite everyone in the congregation to come up with one or two names and addresses of senior adults they personally know. Compile that list of names, and begin making contacts.

6. *Preschool or day schools*—If the church has a preschool, nursery school, or day school, these can be tremendous outlets for reaching seniors. Send senior adult ministry brochures home with all children to give to their families. Ask other Christian schools in your area to distribute fliers too. Their church may not have an active seniors' ministry. This is particularly important as you schedule specific special events geared toward senior adults. Other churches that don't have specialized senior adult ministries are willing to distribute fliers because it provides a service to their families. For example, if you schedule a blood pressure or health-screening day or health fair, seniors from many congregations would be interested.

7. *Community service organizations*—Often a boys and girls club or YMCA is willing to make your senior adult brochure available because your ministry meets special needs. Many times these other organizations are actually looking for referrals. They'll recommend your senior adult ministry. Boy and Girl Scouts, Chamber of Commerce, Welcome Wagon, local schools, and other community organizations provide rich opportunities to distribute brochures and obtain names of potential seniors to invite to your church.

8. *Special event posters in business and local offices*—Have attractive posters printed up, and ask people in your congregation to hang copies in their offices. Ask your junior high and high school youth to take a few hours some afternoon and go store to store asking if the merchants would allow them to hang posters in the store windows. Give specific addresses to the children and teens, or simply have them walk up and down streets in shopping areas. Have some ice cream or pizza after the work to bring a happy ending to a job well done. Plan quarterly major events that have a wide appeal for senior adults. Music or health issues almost always draw a crowd.

CHECKLIST TO HELP IN YOUR OUTREACH PLANNING

As you plan how you'll reach out to the seniors in your community, here's a quick checklist that'll help you cover all the bases.

❑ We have a workable plan for identifying prospects for our senior adult ministry.

❑ Our church has a system of identifying new families that move into the area, and a copy of these contacts is forwarded to the senior adult ministry coordinator.

❑ Prospects are given regular prayer and attention in our senior adult planning.

❑ We have a workable strategy for reaching and winning new senior adult prospects for Christ for our senior adult ministry.

❑ We have a way of regularly encouraging our congregation to provide names of seniors for us to follow up with.

❑ Our church provides regular events outside of Sunday school at which we can obtain names of seniors for our senior adult ministry.

❑ We offer ongoing training to help our people see the importance of outreach to senior adults.

❑ We have a strategy to help bring seniors into our Sunday school and midweek ministries.

❑ We have an active follow-up plan for visitors.

❑ There is a good working relationship in place through which the Sunday school, midweek ministry, and senior adult ministry can coordinate efforts and help each other.

Jesus healed people, and people are still in need of healing—emotionally and spiritually as well as physically.

Remember how Jesus reached people, and use that as an example for senior adult outreach ministry. Jesus took a personal interest in people, not programs. Jesus had compassion for individuals and was never so busy that he couldn't show personal compassion. Jesus healed people, and people are still in need of healing—emotionally and spiritually as well as physically. Jesus dealt with vital problems and met them head-on. Jesus was an inspiration to others, gave good advice, and surprised people. Jesus challenged people to serve and led them to eternal life. What an example for us to follow!

As you think of your senior adult ministry as a strategic outreach tool for your church, use the Vision for Ministry Response Sheet on page 100 to help you chart out your plan in your Sunday school classes, small groups, committees, or boards ten or twelve weeks before the day your outreach is set to begin.

23 HELPFUL HINTS FOR EFFECTIVE OUTREACH

1. *Make them feel welcome.* Name tags can help people feel welcome. With computer technology, you can make personalized visitor name tags in a matter of seconds, or you can purchase blank name tags that visitors simply write their names on when they arrive. What's more important than the name tag is that the visitor feels warmly greeted. Train people in your congregation to be alert to guests and mix and mingle. In informal gatherings, I frequently use phrases such as "mingle" and "get acquainted with several folks you don't already know." Also, in more informal settings, it's always good to provide light refreshments so that people are encouraged to stay and visit with one another.

We have a Sunday night fellowship time at which we serve coffee, punch, and cookies or simple finger food. A "friendship corner" is another excellent way to create fellowship and welcome first-time guests. At the back of our worship center, we actually have created a warm and inviting "corner" with two very comfortable chairs, a love seat, a floor lamp, end tables with literature on them, and a large "friendship corner" sign. We have a monthly host and hostess who are responsible to stay at the friendship corner after worship and not only greet visitors, but also connect first-time guests with others. We highlight the friendship corner at the start of worship and encourage visitors and others to remain there after worship to become better acquainted. Members of the congregation will often ask first-time guests to go out to lunch with them, providing another wonderful opportunity to establish friendships.

2. *Visitor registration card.* Most churches have a visitor registration card, but ours is a little different. Along with general information like name, address, and telephone number, we add an extra spot at the top—

a "phonetically sounds like" line. This can be a helpful aid to whoever is introducing the new guests publicly and for those making home visits. We also ask the visitor to print out his or her name. Of course, some names are difficult to pronounce. In those cases, we ask for their understanding. It's important to have well-trained people staff the welcome area where the cards are being filled out, otherwise the "phonetically sounds like" line will be of little value. (Sample Visitor Registration Card at the end of this chapter.)

3. *Personalized outreach calling cards.* Small "outreach calling cards" are another effective way to make people feel welcome. Immediately after a first visit, people from the church make a telephone call asking if they can come by with a gift. They bring a small gift and leave literature along with the "outreach calling card" that has a spot for the person making the visit to sign his or her name and jot down a personal note. This personalizes the visit and makes yet another positive connection.

4. *Welcome packet envelopes.* We also have a large envelope to put literature in that is taken to the home after first-time visitors attend our church.

5. *"Muggers."* We jokingly have a group in our congregation known as the "Muggers." These are people who take a simple gift to our first-time visitors—a gift of a coffee mug filled with candy kisses. The "Muggers" make their visits early in the week and simply let the first-time guests know that we appreciated their visiting our church.

6. *Visitation assignment slip.* You can make your own or order these through a local Christian bookstore or denomination. What's important is immediate follow-up. First there should be a telephone call asking for a time the callers can make the visit. Then send someone for a brief visit and have him or her leave some literature and a very simple gift (such as a coffee mug or pen). At that visit, the question should be asked if it would be OK for the pastor to come by sometime to get acquainted. Finally, good notes should be kept on the visitation assignment slip. The slip should be given to the pastor or staff person who will properly continue the follow-up process.

7. *Name tag order card.* Have some name tag order forms readily available so that whenever a guest feels that he or she will begin coming regularly to the group, a name tag can be ordered. We have found name tags to be incredibly helpful in our ministry. In fact, many years ago when I was on a large church staff working with college students, I used name tags for collegians. Name tags are helpful in creating community.

8. *Newsletter to visitors for three months.* We have a system by which all guests are automatically put on our newsletter mailing list for three months. If they continue coming, they're informed of important events in which they could be involved. If they do not return, at least they've received a little more information. After three months, however, if they haven't returned, we remove their names.

9. *Sign up to help as greeter or usher.* People love choices. We have a simple clipboard in the foyer that has spots for people to sign up to greet and usher.

10. *Audiocassette or videocassette sign-up sheet.* If your church provides audiotapes or videotapes of the service, provide a simple sign-up sheet or order form. Audiotapes and videotapes are effective ministry tools to homebound or shut-in friends.

11. *Pastor/staff alert cards.* I found long ago that many people leaving worship would make comments to me about illnesses or upcoming surgeries, and then on the drive back home, I would forget the details. The "pastor alert card" is a lifesaver. People simply jot down their information and hand it to me at the door as they leave. Then, as I have opportunity, I can look carefully over the cards and respond. (Sample at back of this chapter.)

12. *Encouragement cards. Stretcher Bearers* by Mike Slater has a great idea in it called "Encouraging One Another" cards.[3] People send notes of encouragement to others in the group. We provide encouragement cards in the seat pockets with the other church information, such as the visitor brochure, offering envelope, and pastor alert cards. We have volunteers regularly keep up the literature in the pockets of the worship center seats. The encouragement cards are another tool to create a feeling of warmth and love. Encourage people to use the cards often. If they don't know the address of someone, we simply say to drop it off by the office and we'll mail the encouragement card. (Sample at back of this chapter.)

13. *Emergency cards.* Emergencies can quickly arise, and you need immediate information on family and friends to notify. We began a card file with members' and friends' vital information, and the file is kept readily available to ushers. Of course, when an emergency happens, the first step is to call 911. After immediate medical needs are met, the emergency card file is then checked. Emergency medical staff greatly appreciate this convenience. You can simply hand them the emergency card, and there is the information they need. (Sample at back of this chapter.)

14. *Prayer cards.* Receiving people's prayer requests can be an effective part of an outreach program. (Sample Prayer Card on page 77.)

15. *Prayer dots.* Some time ago, we showed an "INJOY" video with Dr. John Maxwell. In that video, they encouraged prayer for the pastor. So we started using prayer cards. Someone in our congregation also suggested that we get a roll of small, red dots. We distributed the little dots among the congregation, asking everyone to put a dot on his or her watch. Every time people looked at their watches, they were to breathe a brief prayer for their pastor. What an encouragement for me, as their pastor, to constantly see people with red dots on their watches! This is a good witness tool as well. When someone asks them what the red dots mean, they simply say, "To remind me to pray for my pastor." What a joy to see people praying!

16. *Read through the Bible brochure.* Each year I love to encourage our congregation to join with me in reading through the Bible. You may order Bible reading schedules from the American Bible Society in New York.

17. *"Who Should Make a Will?" seminar.* Everyone who has property of any kind—money, personal possessions, real estate, stocks—and those who care about what ultimately happens to their property should make a will. We have literature available in our foyer. Check with a denominational office for people who can help with estate planning.

18. *Directories including members, friends, and visitors.* It's important to have up-to-date church directories available. With seniors, it may be necessary to have a winter and summer directory. Pictorial directories are great as well.

19. *Worship attendance pads.* We've found that it's best to use attendance registration pads that are passed along rows at the start of worship. (This may seem like a duplication for visitors who fill out a visitor card, but it has proved helpful.) We keep careful attendance of every person and do immediate follow-up of *everyone*—visitors, members, and regular attendees. Sometimes if a visitor arrives a bit late, he or she slips in without filling out the visitor card. However, that person is able to fill out the attendance registration slip as it comes down his or her row.

20. *Inquirers' class sessions.* People who are interested in learning more about our church and its ministries are encouraged to attend the "Pastor's Inquirers' Class." We do everything we possibly can to inform people about our ministries so that they can make an intelligent decision on church membership. Most important is session one: "What It Means to Be a Christian." Session two covers "What We Believe." Session three deals with "What We Practice," and the last session deals with "Who We Are."

21. *Yes, I'd like to become a member.* If someone is interested in becoming a member of our church, there is a form he or she can fill out. It asks the basic information necessary, but it also serves as the "Membership Profile" for service in the future. (Sample at end of this chapter.)

22. *Visitor letter with a self-addressed, stamped comment card.* There are two sample visitor letters at the end of this chapter: one for local visitors, and one for nonresident visitors. One thing we've found to be valuable, however, is to include a self-addressed and stamped comment card for the visitor to fill out and return. (Sample at end of this chapter.)

23. *Friends away from home.* These slips are helpful for seniors who leave for the summer months or during the year for extended travel. (Sample at the back of this chapter.)

I'm a Senior Adult, and I'm New Here

Have you ever wondered what someone thinks who walks into your senior adult group for the first time? If you haven't, you should. Imagine that you're arriving at your church for the first time as a walk-in visitor. Ask yourself the following questions:

Have you ever wondered what someone thinks who walks into your senior adult group for the first time? If you haven't, you should.

- What are your first impressions of the group based on the building, parking lot, and immediate environment?
- What happens when you first enter the building? What are your impressions based on the people you first meet (ushers, members, greeters, children)?
- Do you feel comfortable or uncomfortable as you first come in?
- Are you ignored by most of the people?
- Do you feel like you are wanted, appreciated, cared for? Or is "Welcome!" the first and last word you hear?
- What are your impressions of the worship service? or of the Sunday school Bible study?
- Does there seem to be a spiritual excitement or dynamic within the service or Sunday school class and among the people? Or is the class/ Bible study or service contrived and little more than a series of rituals?
- When the class or service is over, what happens?
- Is it easy to feel like you can become a part of this church, or would it take considerable effort?
- After you have left, do you have any desire or reason or need to come back?
- During the next week, do the pastor or laypersons show any interest in you? Are you thanked for coming to the church? Do you feel as though the "thank you" is personal and meaningful?

SHORT-TERM MISSIONS WITH LONG-TERM IMPACT FOR SENIORS

More and more churches are realizing that senior adults have time, resources, energy, and expertise. It's the job of the church of the twenty-first century to discover the incredible power of short-term missions with long-term impact. Just one week, given in Jesus' name, can make a world of difference.

Just one week, given in Jesus' name, can make a world of difference.

Denominations, mission organizations, and churches are all realizing that seniors are the untapped resource for short-term mission projects. Isaiah 6:8 truly becomes a reality: "Then I heard the voice of the Lord saying, 'Whom shall I send? And who will go for us?' And I said, 'Here am I. Send me!' "

When seniors go on a short-term mission trip, they join with other Christians and begin to live God's love in a way most never dreamed possible. "Let your light shine before men," Jesus says in Matthew 5:16, "that they may see your good deeds and praise your Father in heaven." As short-term teams work together and reach out with compassion, they gain the trust and friendship of those they help, allowing them to share God's love in a natural, effective way.

Seniors involved in short-term mission projects can plan on laughing and learning like never before. Yes, it will involve a great deal of work, but what satisfaction! It's a little risky for seniors because it takes them out of their comfort zone, but most active senior adults actually want that. There's so much more to life than traditional retirement. After the novelty of cruises and travel wears off, seniors tire of earthly pleasures and want more meaning in their retirement.

After the novelty of cruises and travel wears off, seniors tire of earthly pleasures and want more meaning in their retirement.

Those able to travel find the idea of traveling for a worthy project extremely interesting. New friends are made, often with people of a different culture. Most trips involve equal portions of hard work and ministry to children through kids' clubs and other types of outreach ministries.

There is also culture shock. Sometimes there are unrealistic expectations and team conflicts. But the growth that takes place in the life of any senior who participates in a short-term mission trip is staggering. Most denominations can put seniors in touch with short-term mission coordinators. One fine organization is World Servants, 7130 Portland Ave. South, Richfield, MN 55423-3264. Their telephone number is (612) 866-0010, and their fax number is (612) 866-0078.

Habitat for Humanity is another great organization to contact for local outreach and mission projects. (121 Habitat St., Americas, GA 31709; publicinfo@hfhi.org; (229) 924-6935)

SIMPLE IDEAS FOR OUTREACH AT HOME OR ABROAD

Remember the song " 'Tis the Gift to Be Simple"? Here are some very simple ways a senior group can easily get involved in outreach both at home and abroad. Remember, a mission is not always going across the seas; it is often going across the street as well.

A mission is not always going across the seas; it is often going across the street as well.

• *Visiting others*—Encourage seniors to visit homebound friends, those in the hospital, and those in assisted living or nursing homes on a regular basis. Visiting is a simple gift of friendship that costs nothing.

• *Senior Helping Hands*—Picture a group of senior adults scraping and painting a house for a needy family, rebuilding a porch, developing a park, or cleaning up a neighborhood. Select a major project that can be accomplished in four to five workdays, and let the senior adults lead in this community service. How about this becoming an annual event for your seniors' group? You might even include older youth and young adults to make this an intergenerational project. Give lots of positive recognition to those who are involved. Present a service of dedication prior to the project and a brief video or slide presentation to the congregation after the project is complete.

• *Lunch partners*—A lunch partner is assigned to a homebound person and has lunch weekly with that person. Lunch may be brought into the home, or they can go out to eat.

• *Substitute caregivers*—Substitute caregivers stay with an ill or disabled person for a few hours each week, allowing the relative or caregiver a break from responsibility.

• *Beautify the church*—Senior adults love to assume responsibility for improving the church landscape or doing minor remodeling inside. Does a classroom or the library need a fresh coat of paint? How long has it been since the sanctuary pews were cleaned or waxed? What church kitchen doesn't need new shelf paper in the cabinets? Seniors can have a special ministry by tackling the small, neglected tasks that seldom get done.

• *International students*—International students attending college in the United States enjoy visiting in American homes, and they make delightful and fascinating guests.

• *School helpers*—Retired adults find meaningful service in assisting our public or private schools. Special education teachers welcome volunteer assistants in the classroom. Tutoring is also a wonderful way to be involved in outreach.

• *Audiotape delivery*—Expand a homebound ministry by taking the studies done at the church right to the homes of homebound friends. Simply have small portable tape players taken to the homes of homebound seniors, and have seniors deliver audiotapes weekly.

• *VBS*—Seniors love to be involved in vacation Bible school. I used to have what I called my "cookie brigade." This was a group of senior adults who would, at a moment's notice, bake cookies for some event that was planned.

• *Nursing home VBS*—Why not involve senior adults in Bible school by organizing and conducting a VBS in a nursing home? Those in the assisted living or nursing home cannot come to the church, so go to them. Keep it simple. Some singing, short Bible story, refreshments, a simple game, and closing songs are all things you could do. What a wonderful and powerful ministry of outreach!

• *Survey of interests, abilities, and needs*—Try giving a simple survey to your seniors to find out their interests, abilities, and needs. Then you can match abilities with needs. For example, you might include the following categories: transportation, grocery shopping, telephoning homebound persons, visiting homebound persons, cooking, housecleaning, and reading.

• *Transportation*—People who do not drive must have assistance in getting to church, the doctor, the grocery store, and other appointments.

• *Paperwork*—Some seniors can have problems with filling out forms, necessary papers, and tax forms. There may be some active senior adults who would be willing to help others fill out forms.

• *Trips*—Seniors love outings and trips. You can have key seniors help with lining up trips and outings. Bus transportation or car pools and meals are all details that active seniors can be helpful with. You can have day trips, overnight trips, extended weekend trips, or mystery trips.

• *Dial-a-devotion*—You might consider having a telephone line put in just for a daily devotional. Homebound friends can call in and receive a word of encouragement each day via a recorded telephone devotional message. Active seniors can maintain this project.

• *Senior adult day or weekend*—To keep the needs and focus of senior adult ministry before the congregation, try having a senior adult day or weekend. You could plan a service or seminar or devote the entire weekend to seniors.

• *Stephen Ministries*—This is a great church-sponsored ministry. Stephen ministers are trained lay people who provide Christian care to those facing a crisis. (For more about this ministry, visit their Web site: www.stephenministries.org.)

IDEAS FOR OUTINGS AND TRIPS FOR SENIORS

Here are some creative ideas for outings and trips with your senior group:

• appreciation night	• progressive dinners	• videos
• softball	• fast food	• table tennis
• banquet	progressive dinner	• billiards
• barbecue	• ice cream social or	• planetarium
• lake or river trips	ice cream outing	• Polaroid scavenger
• Bible studies	• theater	hunts
• boat cruise	• libraries	• work days/parties
• bowling	• local parks	• scavenger hunts
• events with other	• miniature golf	• tennis
senior groups	• museums	• zoo trips

For other ideas check the local Yellow Pages. Simply looking through the Yellow Pages gives you countless ideas for senior outings.

Remember that an active senior adult is a person who makes the most of his or her age and experience. Senior adults love to be with people and love to serve. They're growing into full maturity in Christ. They love to take an active part in the life of the church and the family of God. They love life and love to live life to its fullest. A key for working with senior adults is found in Philippians 3:13-14: "Forgetting what is behind and straining forward to what is ahead, I press on toward the goal to win the prize for which God has called me heavenward in Christ Jesus." Seniors have such a vital part in the church today as they contribute their time and talent.

Ask yourself these questions as you think of senior adults and outreach ministry:

- What are the special talents and abilities of senior adults I know?
- How can I help senior adults I work with make better use of their time?
- What are their special interests and abilities, and how can I help them utilize these interests and abilities?
- What special knowledge and experience do seniors have that can be shared for the mutual growth and benefit of the entire congregation?

Help seniors understand that their contributions count. Their special gifts are blessings from God that can make a difference. 1 Peter 4:10 says, "Each one should use whatever gift he has received to serve others, faithfully administering God's grace in its various forms." Help seniors contribute in worship, in the community, in church ministries, in social concerns, in teaching, and in all areas of life. Most of all, help seniors realize that one of the greatest ways they can reach out is through prayer.

VISION FOR MINISTRY RESPONSE SHEET

In twelve weeks we will be offering a new (or revitalized) senior adult ministry at our church. The senior adult ministry mission statement is "To reach and to hold more people for Christ and this church in 20__." Matthew 28:19 challenges us to "go and make disciples." We need the help of every Sunday school class, small group, committee, and board of our church to make this senior adult outreach ministry work. Please respond to the following questions and return your completed sheet to the senior adult committee by [date].

1. How does the overall senior adult ministry goal of reaching new people for Christ and incorporating them into the church relate to your individual class or group?

2. What are some specific ways your class or group can help our church achieve the goal of reaching new people for Christ and incorporating them into the church?

3. What steps can you take now to implement the above plans?

4. Brainstorm together the names, addresses, and telephone numbers of any senior adults you know of that we could invite to our seniors' program.

REACHING OUT LIKE JESUS

Look up the following two Scripture passages. Read each and then think of ways Jesus came near, saw, and "felt" the needs of those he came to minister to.

- Matthew 9:35-38
- Luke 19:41

	Ways Jesus responded	**Ways I can respond today**
Jesus came near.		
Jesus saw.		
Jesus wept.		

Following each statement below, jot down ways you and your congregation can help make seniors a high priority in your church:

1. Make outreach a top priority.

2. Provide meaningful outreach opportunities using new and different ways to involve volunteers.

3. Utilize effective ministries of love and caring.

4. Place the focus on spiritual maturity that is not based on knowledge but rather on demonstrated attitude and action.

5. Train leadership and provide program structures that are flexible and consistent.

IMPROVING YOUR RECRUITING

What can you do to make your recruitment process better? Jot down ways and ideas for improvement.

• Ways I can nurture a positive recruitment atmosphere:

• Ways I can promote the needs to the congregation:

• Ways I can help provide clearly written job descriptions:

• Ways I can search prayerfully and carefully for the volunteers I need:

• Ways I can secure approval from the powers that be before I ask someone to serve:

• Ways I can—after prayer, time, and reflection—ask for a decision:

TELECARE MINISTRY CALLING REPORT
(FROM PALM WEST COMMUNITY CHURCH)

Top Portion of Form to Be Completed by Pastoral Staff:

Name of Person to Be Contacted: _____

Phone Number: _____

Frequency of Contact: ❏ Weekly   ❏ Bimonthly   ❏ Monthly

Background:

_____

_____

_____

To Be Completed by Telecare Caller:

Contact #1

Date: _____   Caller's Name: _____

Comments:

_____

_____

Special Prayer Requests:

_____

_____

_____

Pastoral Comments:

_____

_____

_____

Date: _____   Follow-Up Call Necessary? ❏ Yes ❏ No

(continued on next page)

Telecare Ministry Calling Report, p. 2

To Be Completed by Telecare Caller:

Contact #2

Date: _____   Caller's Name: _____

Comments:

_____

_____

Special Prayer Requests:

_____

_____

_____

Pastoral Comments:

_____

_____

_____

Date: _____   Follow-Up Call Necessary? ❏ Yes ❏ No

VISITOR REGISTRATION CARD

MR.
MRS.
MISS_____ DATE _____

PHONETICAL (Sounds Like) _____

ADDRESS_____ APT. _____

CITY _____ STATE _____ ZIP _____

PHONE (___)_____ I AM A GUEST OF _____

HOME CHURCH _____ WHERE _____

❏ Visitor for First Time   ❏ New in Community
❏ Would Like to Know More About Church   ❏ Would Like to Unite With This Church
❏ Would Like Minister to Call

"PASTOR/STAFF ALERT" CARD

"Pastor/Staff Alert" Card

Prayer Request:
☐ Prayer chain | ☐ Pastor only | ☐ Church prayer list

Illness/Hospitalization/Surgery/Health Concern:

Name _____ Concern/Procedure/Surgery _____ Date of procedure _____

Someone in need of a visit from the Pastor:

☐ Home visit would be nice | ☐ Just a telephone call would be fine

Use the back to write out prayer request, note to the Pastor, Music Director, or Secretary for bulletin, Palm West Alive, etc.)

ENCOURAGEMENT CARD

Encouraging One Another

And let us consider how we may spur one another on toward love and good deeds. Let us not give up meeting together, as some are in the habit of doing, but let us encourage one another — and all the more as you see the Day approaching (Hebrews 10:24-25).

Dear _____

_____

_____

_____

_____

_____

             _____

Palm West Community Church
13845 W. Stardust Blvd.
Sun City West, AZ 85375
(602)546-2980

To:

EMERGENCY CARD

Palm West Community Church
Emergency Information Form

Name(s)_____

Home Phone_____

Doctor_____

Doctor Phone No._____

Next of Kin or Responsible Friends

Name_____

Relationship_____

Home Phone No._____

Name_____

Relationship_____

Home Phone No._____

Do you have a "Living Will" in Arizona?_____

Medications_____

_____

_____

Allergies_____

Special Health Problems_____

_____

Blood Type_____

Comments (Use back if necessary)

Please PRINT Name(s)_____

Date____

MEMBERSHIP PROFILE (SIDE 1)

Yes, I Would Like To Become A Member of

Palm West Community Church

Membership Profile

Dr. David P. Gallagher, Senior Pastor

13845 W. Stardust Blvd., Sun City West, AZ 85375
Church Phone: (623) 546-2980

In the space below, please give any additional information that may help us in finding a place of service for you at Palm West. Share what you feel are your spiritual gifts, talents and hobbies that would be helpful for the future of our church ministry:

On behalf of Palm West Community Church, thank you for taking time to share.

Our Mission – is to advance the Kingdom of Jesus Christ. We seek to attain this through public worship of God, the spiritual growth of its members and friends, inviting persons to accept Jesus Christ as Lord and Savior and evangelistic outreach and missionary endeavor.

Our Vision – is to unify together, edify one another and glorify God by reaching people with the Gospel, sharing the plan of salvation, leading them to Christ and discipling them in the Christian faith.

Palm West Community Church
"A Spiritual Oasis in the Desert"

General Areas of Service

Ministry	Have Served in the Past	Willing to Serve
Art/Posters		
Audit Committee		
Choir Singer		
Church Dinners		
Church Newsletter		
Communion Server		
Computer Work		
Decorating		
Drama		
Church Greeter		
Kitchen Helper		
Lawn & Shrubbery		
Lay Counseling		
Librarian		
Maintenance		
Meals to Homebound		
Men's Fellowship		
Nominating Committee		
Office Helper		
Organist		
Other Instrument		
Pianist		
Prayer Group Leader		
Prayer Warrior		
Publicity Work		
Singles		
Soloist		
Sound Equipment		
Sunday School Teacher		
Trip/outing leader		
Usher		
Vision Setting		
Visit Members or New People		
Visit Homebound or Hospital		
Women's Group		
Writing/Editing		

MEMBERSHIP PROFILE (SIDE 2)

Palm West Community Church
Membership Profile
(To be completed by each person in our membership)

Name: _____

Address: _____
Street _____ City _____ State _____ Zip

Summer Address: _____

Local Phone: _____ Summer Phone: _____

E-mail Address: _____

Birthday: ___ Month ___ Day ___ Anniversary: ___ Month ___ Day

Previous Church: _____

Are you a year round resident? ___ Yes ___ No

Area of country in which you lived prior to Sun City West: _____

Number of children or grandchildren: _____

Hobbies/Interests: _____

Church offices held in the Past: _____

Past Professional Services/Employment: _____

Present Involvement at Palm West: _____

What do you like best about Palm West? _____

How and when did you become a Christian? _____

Have you been baptized? _____

How were you baptized? ___ Immersed ___ Sprinkled

Other _____

Which membership would you like? ___ Regular ___ Associate

Check which way you are requesting to come into our membership:

☐ By Profession of Faith and Baptism (Any person making a profession of faith in Jesus Christ as personal Lord and Savior may be admitted upon baptism by immersion).

☐ By Letter of Transfer: (Any person may be admitted by letter of transfer from another Christian church.

Name and address: _____

☐ By Christian Experience: (Any person may be admitted by statement of faith having previously professed Jesus Christ as personal Lord and Savior, and having experienced Christian baptism (not necessarily by immersion).

☐ By Associate membership: Any person may be admitted as an associate member without obtaining a letter of transfer from his/her church.

☐ By Restoration: Any person may be admitted upon personal request and renewed commitment when prior membership in this Church has been terminated for any reason.

Do you have any questions you would like answered by the pastor or church leadership or comments?

Would you like offering envelopes? ___ Yes ___ No

Specific Ministries at Palm West

	Have Served in the Past	Willing to Serve
Bible Study Leader		
Worship Leader Sunday Mornings		
Song Leader		
Shepherd Group Leader		
TeleCare (phone) or Care Ministry		

Elected and Department Chairs at Palm West
(Elected offices for specific terms of office. Job Descriptions available at office)

Office	Have Served in the Past	Willing to Serve
Moderator		
Vice Moderator		
Church Clerk		
Treasurer		
Assistant Treasurer		
Financial Secretary		
Assistant Financial Secretary		
Education Department		
Fellowship Department		
Finance Department		
Music Department		
Outreach Department		
Property Department		
Worship Department		

Comments:

Office Information: PWCC Membership Profile (Revised 9-18-00)

VISITOR COMMENT/RESPONSE CARD

Visitor Comment/Response Card

1. Your first impressions: ___ Positive ___ Negative
2. Your feelings during worship: ___ Comfortable ___ Uncomfortable
3. Greeted warmly: ___ Yes ___ No
4. Were you able to really worship: ___ Yes ___ No
5. Would you return: ___ Yes ___ No
6. Did you enjoy the music: ___ Yes ___ No
7. Was the sermon helpful: ___ Yes ___ No
8. The style of worship: ___ Comfortable ___ Uncomfortable
9. Your religious background: _____

Comments:_____
_____
_____
_____
_____
_____

Name (Optional)

LOCAL VISITOR LETTER

Palm West Community Church
An American Baptist Fellowship

Dr. David P. Gallagher, Senior Pastor
Dr. William P. Kearns, Pastor Emeritus
Mrs. Erdina Fiedler, Director of Music
Mr. Dick Parsons, Pastoral Assistance Team Coordinator

A Spiritual Oasis in the Desert

February 11, 2002

«Title» «FirstName» «LastName»
«Address1»
«City», «State» «PostalCode»

Dear «FirstName»,

Thanks for visiting us at Palm West Community Church. We are honored that you chose our church in which to worship and fellowship. Palm West is a happy and blessed congregation. I trust that you sensed our joy and felt at home in our midst.

Our purpose is to present the Gospel to those with whom we come in contact with. We often say that our goal is *To Know Christ and make Him Known*. We do this through preaching, teaching, music, praise and through mission and outreach. We have two Sunday morning Worship Services, one at 8:30 am and the second at 10:00 am. We also have a Sunday Morning Bible Study which is held in our Library during both morning services and Sunday Evening Fellowship is held at 6:00 p.m.

On the first Sunday of each month I lead an *Inquirer's Class* that meets from 4:00 p.m. – 5:30 p.m. in the Choir Room. Please come visit the *Inquirer's Class* so we may get better acquainted and so that you may learn more about the ministries of Palm West.

Our Wednesday midweek service is a time of singing; study of the Scriptures and prayer together. On Wednesday night we meet in the Choir Room at 6:00 p.m.

Palm West is a loving fellowship of believers, *the end of your search for a friendly Christ Centered Church*. If I can assist you in any way, please let me know.

Would you take a few moments and fill out and return the enclosed postcard to give us your impressions of your worship experience at Palm West? I thank you in advance for you help in this. Again, welcome to Palm West Community Church! I look forward to seeing you again soon!

Warmly in the Love of Christ,

Dr. David P. Gallagher, D. Min.
Senior Pastor

13845 W Stardust Blvd., Sun City West, AZ 85375
Phone (623) 546-2980 ✳ Fax: (623) 546-9977 ✳ E-mail: drdavog@msn.com

Our Mission – *is to advance the Kingdom of Jesus Christ. We seek to attain this through public worship of God, the spiritual growth of its members and friends, inviting persons to accept Jesus Christ as Lord and Savior and evangelistic outreach and missionary endeavor.*
Our Vision – *is to unify together, edify one another and glorify God by reaching people with the Gospel, sharing the plan of salvation, leading them to Christ and discipling them in the Christian faith.*

NONRESIDENT VISITOR LETTER

Palm West Community Church
An American Baptist Fellowship

Dr. David P. Gallagher, Senior Pastor
Dr. William P. Kearns, Pastor Emeritus
Mrs. Erdina Fiedler, Director of Music
Mr. Dick Parsons, Pastoral Assistance Team Coordinator

A Spiritual Oasis in the Desert

February 11, 2002

Dear,

To our delight, you worshipped with us while you were in Sun City West. We were thankful and honored that you chose our church to visit.

Palm West Community Church is a happy and blessed congregation. I trust you sensed our joy and felt at home.

Our purpose is to present the Gospel, to those we come in contact with. We often say that our purpose is *To Know Christ and to make Him Known*. We do this through preaching, teaching, music, praise and through missions and outreach.

If you are ever in this area in the future please visit us again. We are looking forward to seeing you again soon! Palm West is *"A Spiritual Oasis in the Desert"*!

Warmly in the Love of Christ,

Dr. Dave

Dr. David P. Gallagher, D.Min.
Senior Pastor

13845 W Stardust Blvd., Sun City West, AZ 85375
Phone (623) 546-2980 ✱ Fax: (623) 546-9977 ✱ E-mail: drdavog@msn.com

Our Mission – *is to advance the Kingdom of Jesus Christ. We seek to attain this through public worship of God, the spiritual growth of its members and friends, inviting persons to accept Jesus Christ as Lord and Savior and evangelistic outreach and missionary endeavor.*
Our Vision – *is to unify together, edify one another and glorify God by reaching people with the Gospel, sharing the plan of salvation, leading them to Christ and discipling them in the Christian faith.*

OUR FRIENDS AWAY FROM HOME

If you are going to be away for an extended period, please fill out this slip and place it in the secretary's basket on the counter (just inside the church office door).

Name: _____

Leaving the Sun Cities area on: _____
                                                    Date

Anticipate returning to this area on: _____
                                                    Date

Summer address:

_____

_____

_____

Telephone number where you may be reached if necessary:

_____

Would you like to receive the weekly church bulletin? _____

Would you like to receive the monthly Palm West Alive Newsletter? _____

Would you like to receive the Pastor's summer letter sent to our friends away from home? _____

Please know that we will be praying for you while you are away. If you would be willing to send us a postcard or note, Dr. Dave will read your note to the congregation Sunday morning, and we will post the cards and notes on a bulletin board for our church family to read. Keep us informed of your activities. We love you!

Dr. Dave Gallagher

CHAPTER 5

THE SERIOUS SIDE OF SENIOR ADULT MINISTRY

There's a serious side to senior adult ministry. Anyone who has ever worked with or known senior adults knows that dealing with grief, pain, suffering, and loss is part of the territory. This is the downside of working with seniors.

"Fifty percent of Americans over age 65 suffer from arthritis; 40 percent have high blood pressure; 33 percent have a significant hearing loss; 25 percent have heart disease."[1]

It has been said that we don't "do death well." Most people don't like to think or talk about dying. If you visit a mortuary, you'll hear staff giving happy names to sad things. You'll hear pleasant phrases like "slumber rooms" and bodies being referred to as "remains." Ashes will be called "cremains," and funeral directors will seldom even use the word *death*. Many think that if we don't talk about death, it won't happen. Senior adults, however, know that death will happen. Simply put, "the death rate is one each!" Someone once said, "The leading cause of death is life."[2]

As you think of ways to minister to active seniors, be sure to also think of ways to minister to those who are suffering and experiencing pain and loss. I recently conducted two funerals: one of a husband and then, a year later, the man's wife. The wife's funeral was in the same month as her husband's. At the wife's memorial service, I shared thoughts from a poem by Robert Frost, *Wild Grapes*. In that poem, Frost talks about wisdom. The first part of wisdom, according to Frost, is to

The first part of wisdom is to learn to let go with the hands. The second is to learn what to hold on to with the heart. learn to let go with the hands. The second is to learn what to hold on to with the heart. Sometimes in working with our seniors, we must learn to let go with the hands and learn what to hold on to with the heart.

As we minister to older senior adults who are coming to the close of their lives' journeys, it's important that we help them understand the various steps to peace during life's losses. We begin our fears of death at a very early age. Children talk about ghosts, death, and the unknown. Oddly enough, with our fear and avoidance of death, we at the same time seem to have a fascination with death and dying.[3] We learn early on that grief is bad and something to fear and avoid. But the Bible has a completely different view of death and grief.

Is There "Good Grief"?

Can grief actually be good? One of the first funerals I conducted was of a young man whose life's desire was to be a Marine. After only a week in active military service, he was shot and killed. His body was flown back to the States. I'll never forget his grieving parents as the flag was draped over the casket. Their question haunted my mind as they asked, "Why?"

On Christmas Eve, 1977, I received a telephone call from a hospital. The call was from parents of a junior high boy who had accidentally shot himself in the eye. Their son was in emergency surgery. Can there be any good in that kind of grief?

We can learn that through our own grief, we can become instruments of God and his grace. Psalm 91 is a psalm of comfort. We can learn that through our own grief, we can become instruments of God and his grace.

5 Good Things Hidden in Grief

1. There is good in our grief when we understand that our feelings and our timelines differ. Psalm 91:1 reminds us that "he who dwells in the shelter of the Most High will rest in the shadow of the Almighty." People respond to grief in different ways. Grief can be something as horrible as a catastrophe, such as the loss of a spouse, child, grandchild, or close friend. Grief can also be experienced when we're in a financial crisis, moving to a new community, having to make new friends, or having disappointments in our lives because our children or grandchildren did not go in the direction we prayed they would. Death, divorce, marital separation, physical sickness, and injury all cause grief. Yes, even retirement can bring grief.

Edgar Jackson described grief in this way: "Grief is a young widow who must seek a means to bring up her three children, alone. Grief is the angry reaction of a man so filled with shocked uncertainty and confusion that he strikes out at the nearest person...Grief is a mother walking daily to a nearby cemetery to stand quietly and alone for a few moments before she goes on about the tasks of the day; she knows that part of her is in the cemetery, just as part of her is in her daily work...Grief is the silent, knife-like terror and sadness that comes a hundred times a day, when you start to speak to someone who is no longer there. Grief is the emptiness that comes when you eat alone after eating with another for many years. Grief is teaching yourself somehow to go to bed without saying good night to the one who has died. Grief is the helpless wishing that things were different when you know they are not and never will be again. Grief is a whole cluster of adjustments, apprehensions and uncertainties that strike life in its forward progress and make it difficult to...redirect the energies of life."[4] That's grief.

2. There can be good in our grief when we realize that the "stages of grieving" often blend and merge together. Psalm 91:2 says, "I will say of the Lord, 'He is my refuge and my fortress, my God, in whom I trust.' " The stages we go through in the grieving process are shock, denial, resentment, anger, acceptance, and readjustment. It's easy to understand these stages academically, in our heads. We can think through these reactions. But to experientially move through these stages is a whole different issue. And what makes it more difficult is that the phases and stages are not clear-cut. The stages of grief differ from person to person. The goal is to accept the fact that God is our refuge and our fortress.

3. There can be good in our grief when we remember that God is always with us and covers us. Psalm 91:3-8 says, "Surely he will save you from the fowler's snare and from the deadly pestilence. He will cover you with his feathers, and under his wings you will find refuge; his faithfulness will be your shield and rampart. You will not fear the terror of night, nor the arrow that flies by day, nor the pestilence that stalks in the darkness, nor the plague that destroys at midday. A thousand may fall at your side, ten thousand at your right hand, but it will not come near you. You will only observe with your eyes and see the punishment of the wicked." Have you ever watched a mother protect her child? Have you ever seen cats, chickens, or birds with their little ones? The mother bird covers her tiny baby birds with her wings. They find refuge in the mother's faithfulness. "He will cover you with his feathers, and under his wings you will find refuge; his faithfulness will be your shield and rampart."

4. There can be good in our grief when we let it open a door of opportunity to help someone else. Psalm 91:9-12 says, "If you make the Most High your dwelling—even the Lord, who is my refuge—then no harm will befall you, no disaster will come near your tent. For he will command his angels concerning you to guard you in all your ways; they will lift you up in their hands, so that you will not strike your foot against a stone." Hebrews 13:5b says, "Never will I leave you; never will I forsake you."

Grief is often associated with a loss because of death. But grief can be the loss of a relationship. I remember all too well when our son and daughter, both wonderful children who love the Lord, went through a devastation that tore our lives apart. You'll understand as you read a letter I wrote to our family members and friends. The letter told the facts of how deep the pain penetrated, but more importantly, the letter reminds us all that grief is not just death, and no one is exempt from tragedy. On a warm Memorial Day afternoon, I sat at my computer and began to pray and write:

Dear Friends,

We have something very personal to share with you that has touched our lives deeply. We have not shared this sooner because we both were too emotionally involved and because we felt that we were too new in the ministry here. My wife and I have felt that God called us to serve and minister to *you*, not for you to carry our burdens. However, in a few weeks, I will come to my first anniversary as your pastor. We both feel your loyalty, love, and support so strongly in our lives now. Thus, we now share with you our pain at this time.

God has given us two wonderful children. We have raised them to be committed Christians. Both have served the Lord in many ways over the years. Both are loving, caring, and sensitive. Both love the Lord and have a personal relationship with Christ. Both have grown up in the church and gone to Sunday school, children's church, summer and winter camps, vacation Bible school, and on the list goes. We have given our family the highest priority in our lives. We thank God for our two wonderful children and for God's grace in their lives.

But there are things that happen in life that we do not understand, nor do we control. Some of you have learned this already. Satan is alive and actively seeking to destroy. We have felt led by the Lord to share a very personal tragedy that has come into our lives in this regard.

Our son was married on August 8. Rod was a student at a seminary. He met a wonderful young woman who was a student, too, at another seminary close by. They felt a deep love for each other and, after some months, announced their engagement and their plans to marry.

They saw a marriage counselor for their premarital counseling. The next question was who would do their wedding since they both had family and friends in ministry. They decided to have three ministers preside at their wedding. The pastor of the evangelical church where our son was youth pastor, a seminary professor who was a good friend of our son's fiancée and, of course, yours truly. All three of us, along with their marriage counselor, agreed they would both do well in their marriage. We performed the marriage ceremony that year.

My wife and I grew to love this new bride as a special daughter-in-law. She was reserved and businesslike, but very professional and seemed to have a deep love for our son. We felt that the two of them would do just fine. Shortly after the wedding, they moved out of state. They both had excellent jobs.

Our son's new wife had experienced some trauma and grief that we were unaware of. This levied a heavy toll on the new marriage relationship.

Pressures of these unsettled issues, married life, job, and career all caused great stress on the marriage. Our son and daughter-in-law began seeing a marriage counselor. In the midst of this, she announced her intent to separate. Our son continued to see a marriage counselor. Satan gained a victory in that a divorce followed.

But the sorrow and grief does not end there. Our daughter was married in the same year as our son. She and her fiancée had good jobs. They met through a mutual friend, and their relationship began to grow. He seemed to be the perfect person for our daughter. My wife and I grew to love him deeply. We had a big wedding with all the trimmings. Everything about the wedding was beautiful and seemed so perfect. I did the premarital counseling and went the extra mile. Not only did we have the normal six sessions, but also extra testing to make sure this was a solid relationship. We felt very comfortable with their relationship. In fact, I was overwhelmed with the quality of this man my daughter had fallen in love with.

After the wedding they moved to Phoenix. But this young man, too, had experienced some difficulties in life that we were unaware of.

Some months into the marriage, he began to spend extra long hours at work. They began seeing a marriage counselor.

He finally announced that he wanted a separation and moved out. Our daughter continued seeing the marriage counselor alone. She saw a pastor weekly for support and guidance. They divorced, and lives were changed forever.

During the past two years, we have gone through the most difficult time of our lives. When God led us to this church, Satan tried to defeat us. There were times of loneliness and frustration in leaving lifelong friends. We moved to a new city and new ministry knowing that God had led us. Satan tried hard to discourage us. But when Satan could not destroy our vision and confidence in our call to serve God, he chose to attack our children. There is no doubt in our minds that Satan is at the root of this tragedy.

During those difficult days, our daughter would call us three and four times a day crying and asking, "Why?" The pain was deeper than anything we had ever experienced. I did the funeral for both my mother and my father, and the pain was not as deep as this. Being a new pastor, we did not feel the liberty to share our sorrow with anyone but God and each other.

It was during the same time that our son called us often in tears over his life falling apart and his dreams turning to ashes. We are two thousand miles away from both of our children. One Tuesday morning specifically, I recall our son's telephone call to me at the church office. As he was driving, he was on a cellular telephone, crying, asking me "Why?" and asking God "Why?"

We, too, have found ourselves at the foot of the cross asking our loving Father, "Why?" The words to the William Gaither song "Something Beautiful" have had special meaning to us.

It has taken us this long to gain the strength to share some of our feelings with our friends. *You* are part of that special group. We would have given our own lives rather than see and feel the hurt and pain that our children have gone through in this. We've read all the books, listened to all the tapes, and found ourselves alone at the foot of the cross, trusting in our Lord.

We know God is with our two children. His strength is sufficient to meet their needs and ours. For our two children, we claim Jeremiah 29:11, 13: "For I know the plans I have for you,' declares the Lord, '...plans to give you hope and a future...You will seek me and find me when you seek me with all your heart.' "

5. There can be good in our grief when it helps us readjust our priorities and focus on God, his love, and his Word. Psalm 91:13-16 says, "You will tread upon the lion and the cobra; you will trample the great lion and the serpent. 'Because he loves me,' says the Lord, 'I will rescue him; I will protect him, for he acknowledges my name. He will call upon me, and I will answer him; I will be with him in trouble, I will deliver him and honor him. With long life will I satisfy him and show him my salvation.' " Grief can help us readjust our priorities. Grief has a way of helping us acknowledge his name. Grief draws us back to our Lord, his love, and his Word. Looking back on my own life, each time I have experienced grief, there have been great lessons to be learned. God never promised an easy journey, but God did promise to be with us through it all. By the grace of God, we grow through our trials, gain strength, and become stronger persons as a result. Grief helps us readjust our priorities and focus on God and God alone.

SUMMARY: GRIEF CAN BE GOOD WHEN...

- We understand that our feelings and our timelines differ.
- We realize that the stages of grieving often blend and merge together.
- We remember that God is always with us and covers us.
- We let it open a door of opportunity to help someone else.
- We let our hearts help to readjust our priorities and focus on God.

4 MISUNDERSTANDINGS ABOUT GRIEF

1. Memory. Perhaps the first misunderstanding about grieving is related to memory. Most of us think it hurts too much to remember a painful experience. In so thinking, we try to cover up the reality of the loss. Years ago, when I conducted a funeral, I would use words that would lessen the impact of the reality that the loved one had "died." I am not suggesting that we be insensitive; quite the contrary. I am suggesting that we be extremely sensitive, but not misleading. The reality is that someone is dying or has died. We come for comfort. We come to reflect upon that person's life. We come not to forget but to remember. "Grief is not a process of forgetting, it is a process of learning to cope while we remember."[5]

Sometimes in working with seniors, we must help them learn to let go with the hands but also help them learn to hold on to precious memories with their hearts. It's important that we keep those two factors in proper perspective: what to let go of and what to hold on to. Memory becomes an important part of that process. When working with senior adults, we'll need to help them learn to let go with their hands. We will need to help them let go of the physical being. But equally important, we will need to help them hold on to the wonderful memories with their hearts. Letting go and holding on are very important parts of the grieving process.

> **We come for comfort. We come to reflect upon that person's life. We come not to forget but to remember. "Grief is not a process of forgetting, it is a process of learning to cope while we remember."**

2. "Grief is an enemy to be avoided." The second misunderstanding about grief is that grief is an enemy. Grief is actually a friend that brings healing. Grief is a positive force for healing. Grief is *not* something to be feared and avoided.[6]

Some years ago I conducted a funeral for an elderly woman and could not help but notice a young grandson who was in perfect emotional control throughout the entire service. He seemed to show no emotion whatsoever. I was interested in how or why he would be seemingly so emotionally detached. However, when the service concluded at the graveside, he slowly and quietly walked away quite a distance. While everyone was quietly reflecting on the life that had been memorialized, I kept a steady eye on the young man. He walked further and further away until at one point, he dropped to his knees. I watched him reach his hands to the sky, and I heard a yell of release that turned into wailing. He was finally beginning to grieve. A major misunderstanding we sometimes face is that grief is our enemy to be avoided. In reality, grief is a dear friend.

3. Denial. A third misunderstanding we sometimes have is that if we do not talk about grief, it will go away. Actually the opposite is true. "Grief that is left to fester often exemplifies itself in some of the things we call social problems." People go through grief in different ways and on different timelines. Women will often enter grief immediately while men will hold back and deny and avoid their feelings. Sometimes these simple differences can drive a wedge between friends or even family members.[7] As we minister to senior adults and help them deal with losses in life, we must help them face reality. We must sensitively and lovingly listen and guide grieving people toward a loving relationship with our Lord.

> **As we minister to senior adults...we must sensitively and lovingly listen and guide grieving people toward a loving relationship with our Lord.**

4. Sympathy. A fourth misunderstanding is that sometimes sympathy makes it worse.[8] I could hardly believe my ears at a ministerial breakfast one morning. One of the church members from another church in the community had visited our morning worship service. We have an excellent follow-up ministry, so I became aware of this elderly man immediately. Learning that he had recently lost his wife but that he was an active member of another church, I hesitated to make a home visit. Instead, I decided to contact the senior pastor of his church. After a week went by, I wondered if the elderly man would be back in our worship service. You guessed it, the next week he was back in worship. At this point, I felt compelled to talk with the elderly man's pastor. When I met with the pastor at a ministerial breakfast and shared with him that one of his members was in worship two Sundays, I was shocked at his response. To my amazement, the pastor used a phrase that surprised me: "crybaby." Indeed the man was extremely emotional, but for good reason. The man was in desperate need of love, caring, and sympathy. He needed help in the grieving process. In many cases, we misunderstand the healing process in thinking that people should get over it.

I have found it helpful to encourage people to understand that loss, and death in particular, is better understood as a transition. When we realize that life is limited, we can get on with *living* to a maximum. The Apostle

Paul wrote about death for the believer as a transition. In 1 Thessalonians 4:13-18 he wrote, "Brothers, we do not want you to be ignorant about those who fall asleep, or to grieve like the rest of men, who have no hope. We believe that Jesus died and rose again and so we believe that God will bring with Jesus those who have fallen asleep in him. According to the Lord's own word, we tell you that we who are still alive, who are left till the coming of the Lord, will certainly not precede those who have fallen asleep. For the Lord himself will come down from heaven, with a loud command, with the voice of the archangel and with the trumpet call of God, and the dead in Christ will rise first. After that, we who are still alive and are left will be caught up together with them in the clouds to meet the Lord in the air. And so we will be with the Lord forever. Therefore encourage each other with these words."

For the Christian, and for the non-Christian, dying is a transition. We are moving from the physical to the spiritual.

Dying involves saying goodbye to a loved one. It's a time of letting go. It's a time of remembering. Dying "rituals" allow people time to face the transition that is before them. These rituals give people dignity and preparation.

There is a wonderful little book, *The Gift of Significance*, written by Doug Manning, in which he carefully outlines these important steps of transition. Manning tells us there is no need to whisper things as our loved one comes closer to the transition of leaving this physical earth; that person is very aware of that fact. The issue is not *whether* they should know. The issue is *"Can we face it with them?"* Tossing Scriptures at sick people does not help. Even "saying a prayer" often leaves an emptiness. True caring on a felt level is what is most helpful.

The issue is not *whether* they should know. The issue is *"Can we face it with them?"*

I remember all too well the experience of my father dying. I was in a church in northern California. My parents were in southern California, living in retirement. I had received news that my dad was very ill. We had visited my parents numerous times. I knew the family doctor. I felt comfortable that when the critical time arrived, I would have time to spend closing hours with my dad. However, one day when I called the hospital to talk with my dad, the nurse told me that he was in a coma. I insisted that she place the telephone receiver next to his ear. She reminded me that he had not responded to anyone or anything for a day or two. When she placed the telephone receiver next to his ear and I said, "Dad, how are you?" I heard these words: "David, is that *you?*" Those were the last words he spoke.

My wife and I quickly drove down to visit Dad in the hospital, only to realize that we were too late. A close friend was there with me in the hospital. I had mentored this young seminary student and guided him as he followed God's calling into full-time ministry. He stood by my side in the hospital room, but he remained totally quiet. As we left the hospital room, he didn't say a word. As we walked down the long hospital corridor, still no word was spoken. As we stepped into the elevator, we were silent. Not one word was spoken, even during the long walk out of the lobby across the parking lot to the car. His arm was around me. When we reached the car, I looked at him and quietly whispered, "Thank you, my friend."

We must pray, yes, but we must learn to be sensitive to the Spirit's leading. We must allow people time to deal with their feelings. We must allow those who are grieving to talk about their feelings. Hospice is a wonderful ministry because it allows people to move through the transition of dying with dignity. I have learned something about clergy: Too often clergy are more interested in conversation and conversion than they are in comfort. Perhaps this is because we have such strong biblical and theological convictions. We have the answers. We have hope to offer the hopeless. We have a message to present to those in need. But often we present that message inappropriately or at the wrong time. It hurts so much to talk and to remember, but it hurts much more to remember and *not* talk.

SOME REMINDERS

- Grief is not an enemy.
- People need permission to grieve.
- Grief takes time. It is *not* wallowing; it usually lasts two years.

It has been said that "Grief is like peeling an onion; it comes off one layer at a time, and you cry a lot."[9]

Divorce, death, miscarriage, suicide, broken relationships and friendships, moving to a new city, a job change: All of these transitions take time for healing. The well-known steps of recovery—shock, anger, resentment, and readjustment—become extremely important in helping people through loss.

The reconstruction process is time-consuming, and we need a lot of patience during this process. We're helping people move on. We're helping them reestablish their lives. We're taking broken lives and fostering healing.

This means that we, too, must learn to cope in a new way. We must help those who are grieving to cope in new ways. We must help people understand that it's important that they remember. In our senior adult ministry, we are not trying to help people forget loved ones. We're trying to help them live with the loved ones not being here. There is a big difference. In all of this we must know when to be available and when to hug. We must know when to talk and when to be silent. We must know when they're feeling happy and when they're feeling sad. For this reason, at our church we have begun a specific ministry called the "Care Ministry." The Care Ministry not only sends flowers and cards but also provides food and friendship. More important, this ministry continues on when the family members have all left to go back home and the house is empty. The real ministry of caring begins when everyone has left and the house is quiet.

In our senior adult ministry, we are not trying to help people forget loved ones. We're trying to help them live with the loved ones not being here.

Doug Manning says, "Grief only comes in one size—extra large."[10] He goes on to point out that there are two important events in grief and pain:

- When the pain starts.
- When the person decides to do something about the pain.[11]

George Marshal came up with a three-step formula for dealing with conflict due to grief: Let the other person tell their story. Let the other person tell their *whole* story. Let the other person tell their whole story *first.*[12] In grief, listen; let the person tell their story. "After all of the books have been read, the seminars experienced, and the speeches heard, someone must reach out and touch."[13]

"Several years ago a government-sponsored study discovered that when people had personal problems, only 28 percent of them went to professional counselors or clinics. Approximately 29 percent consulted their family physician and 42 percent sought help from clergymen. Little wonder that doctors are overworked and pastors are swamped with impossible caseloads—so much so that thousands of needy people are doing what they have done for centuries—turning to friends for advice and encouragement in times of need."[14]

Caring for and helping others is mentioned many times in the Bible. Consider, for example, some of the ways in which God helps people. Look up the following passages, and note the ways in which God helps.

Psalm 46:1

Hebrews 4:16

Hebrews 13:6

Proverbs 3:5-6

Isaiah 40:31

Philippians 4:19

God often uses us to help others. The Bible even commands that we be dedicated people helpers. For example, look up the following verses, and jot down what we are expected to do when people around us are in need.

Matthew 10:8

Romans 12:15

Romans 12:20

Galatians 6:2

1 John 3:17

According to the Bible, it's imperative that Christians reach out to and love others. A first step to being an effective caring and loving person is to invite Christ into our lives to live there and control us: "Dear friends, let us love one another, for love comes from God. Everyone who loves has been born of God and knows God. Whoever does not love does not know God, because God is love" (1 John 4:7-8).

6 Principles of Caring

1. Caring involves a combination of different personalities, values, attitudes, and beliefs.

2. Caring includes attitude, motivation, and a desire to show concern.

3. Caring involves relationships between people in need of help and people who can offer help.

4. Caring must focus on emotions, thoughts, and behavior.

5. Caring involves a variety of skills. There will need to be good listening, sensitive leading, healthy support, occasional confrontation, and frequent teaching.

6. Caring has the goal of pointing people to the Lord himself.[15]

Caring Through Listening

Here are fourteen principles to help you become a better listener.

1. We must be ready to listen.

2. We must guard against judging the person we are listening to.

3. We must control our own emotions.

4. We must resist distractions.

5. We must really pay attention.

6. We must think hard and work to listen between the lines.

7. We must learn to ask good questions. Some questions can get us off track.

8. We must not interrupt.

9. We must stay on the subject.

10. We must use the other person's words to get a point across (reflective listening, "What I think I have heard *you* say is...").

11. We must not give a sermon.

12. We must be quick to hear and slow to speak.

13. We must not argue.

14. We must not ask questions simply to satisfy our curiosity.[16]

WHEN THINGS ARE DOWN, LOOK UP!

I read about a little girl who was dying of leukemia. She asked the nurse for a crying doll. When the nurse asked why, she replied, "Mommy and I need to cry. Mommy won't cry in front of me, and I can't cry if Mommy doesn't. If we had a crying doll, all three of us could cry together. I think we'd feel better."

Psalm 73 is about looking up when things are down. This psalm gives us some practical help on how to help senior adults who are discouraged, depressed, and facing loss and grief. (An encouraging resource for applying this psalm is Ray Stedman's *Folk Psalms of Faith.*[17]) In Psalm 73, the psalmist gives seven practical suggestions for looking up when we're down:

1. *We must be quiet and realize that we simply don't understand.* Psalm 73:15-16 says, "If I had said, 'I will speak thus,' I would have betrayed your children. When I tried to understand all this, it was oppressive to me." Sometimes we simply don't understand why we're going through a situation. Our response must be as the opening verse of this psalm: "Surely God is good to Israel, to those who are pure in heart."

2. *We must help our senior adults to look up into the presence of God.* Psalm 73:17 says, "Till I entered the sanctuary of God; then I understood their final destiny." Sometimes we must look into the presence of a God who is all-powerful and simply realize that God knows and we do not.

When we come into the presence of God, we can relax in God's hands. He is in control when we are not. Sometimes God uses these experiences of allowing us to be down so that we will look up.

3. *We must look up to see the big picture and not lose perspective.* Psalm 73:18-20 says, "Surely you place them on slippery ground; you cast them down to ruin. How suddenly are they destroyed, completely swept away by terrors! As a dream when one awakes, so when you arise, O Lord, you will despise them as fantasies." God sees the big picture. We must not lose perspective. As Martin Luther said, "Without [trials] a person can neither know Scripture or faith, nor can he fear and love God.

When we come into the presence of God, we can relax in God's hands. He is in control when we are not.

If he has never suffered, he cannot understand what hope is." We must look up, be quiet, and realize that we simply do not understand. Look up into the presence of God. Look up to see the big picture and not lose perspective.

4. *We must look up and re-evaluate our thinking.* Psalm 73:21-22 says, "When my heart was grieved and my spirit embittered, I was senseless and ignorant; I was a brute beast before you." How many of the seniors we are working with have "been there, done that"? Bitterness is a reality of life when grief overtakes us. Pain and suffering do strange things to people. We begin to question God. It's easy to become angry. It's easy to begin asking "why" questions. We must help our senior adults look up and re-evaluate their thinking.

5. *We must look up and realize that God still loves us.* Psalm 73:23-24 says, "Yet I am always with you; you hold me by my right hand. You guide me with your counsel, and afterward you will take me into glory." God will guide with counsel. Then we can say afterward, "*You* will take me to glory!"

A pastor friend had just received news of a terminal illness. That next Sunday he told his congregation the news. He had walked five miles from the doctor's office to his home. He had sat looking at the mountains. He had looked at giant trees and the river and the big blue sky. He had said out loud, "I may not see you long, but I'll be alive. River, I'll be alive after you are dry. Trees, I will be alive when you have fallen. Hope lies beyond the grave!" Death is not the end. Innumerable, indescribable, eternal glories are ahead for those who know the Lord!

6. *We must look up and call out for God himself.* Psalm 73:25-26 says, "Whom have I in heaven but you? And earth has nothing I desire besides you. My flesh and my heart may fail, but God is the strength of my heart and my portion forever."

We must remind our senior adults that God in fact does love us. God wants us to love him and to follow him and to trust him.

7. *We must look up and remember that he keeps his word.* Psalm 73:27-28 says, "Those who are far from you will perish; you destroy all who are unfaithful to you. But as for me, it is good to be near God. I have made the Sovereign Lord my refuge; I will tell of all your deeds."

I'm an avid Arizona Diamondbacks fan. One of my favorite expressions is "the ballgame's not over yet." In working with seniors, we must constantly be reminded of that. The psalmist reminds us that we will not perish. We must join with the psalmist, saying, "It is good to be near God. I have made the Sovereign Lord my refuge" (Psalm 73:28). God is faithful. Look up and remember that God is still on the throne. God *is* indeed in full control. When things are down, look up!

KEEPING A HEAVENLY PERSPECTIVE

Depression is a loss of pleasure and enjoyment in life. It's a feeling of sadness, disappointment, and being totally alone. Depression can be physical discomfort, aches, pains, fatigue, poor digestion, and sleep disorder. *Webster's* defines it as that which causes you to sink or be low in spirit; to be sad, dejected, lowering of activity and vitality and mood swings. Depression is a withdrawal from people activities.

At some time everyone experiences a little depression. We feel down on life and down on ourselves. Sometimes after a bad day or a bad golf game, our moods change briefly. Sometimes depression lingers on. We sometimes just can't seem to get back up and shake it off.

Some depression involves what's going on inside, and some involves what's going on outside. Chemical imbalance in the brain can cause depression. Life events can trigger depression. And the death of a loved one, a strained relationship, drugs, a transition, or even the birth of a baby or grandchild can cause depression and deep grief. When we experience depression, we need help—help from God, his Word, and our friends. Sometimes we need help from a pastor, counselor, or physician.

Seniors who are depressed or experiencing grief need people who really care. The Bible tells of David and how he experienced fear. In Psalms 42 and 43, the psalmist writes about depression. There seems to be a cycle of depression. The cycle begins with thoughts and moves on to feelings. The thoughts that caused the feelings create a mood, and the mood sets an attitude and action. When we think silly, happy thoughts, we begin to smile. If we think of a sad event and begin to think negatively, we begin to feel depressed. Negative thoughts cause emotional turmoil. Nearly all of the time, such thoughts are distortions.

I may think I did a terrible job at something, but, in reality, my performance was just fine. Bad feelings are the result of distorted, negative thinking. Our thoughts determine our feelings, our feelings set our moods, and our moods cause our actions. You feel the way you do right now because of thoughts you are thinking right now.

Our thoughts determine our feelings, our feelings set our moods, and our moods cause our actions.

I love to be with happy, positive people. I do not enjoy being around cranky, negative people. Why? Because the moods of others directly affect my moods. Philippians 4:8 says, "Finally, brothers, whatever is true, whatever is noble, whatever is right, whatever is pure, whatever is lovely, whatever is admirable—if anything is excellent or praiseworthy—think about such things."

David applied some basic and simple principles to his life in dealing with depression. Psalm 42 helps us with some of these principles.

---

1. *David remembered how God had helped in the past.* Psalm 42:4, 6 says, "These things I remember as I pour out my soul...therefore I will remember." As we help senior adults who are depressed, lonely, and experiencing grief, we need to help them remember when they were happy. I have wonderful memories from every congregation in which I've served. I keep the wonderful memories before me through pictures in albums and those hanging on a wall in my study. I save the precious notes, letters, and cards that have been given to me over the years. David remembered how God had helped him in the past. We must help our senior adults remember how God has cared for them in the past.

2. *David practiced hope and praise, even during times of discouragement.* Psalms 42:5-6a, 11; 43:5 say, "Why are you downcast, O my soul? Why so disturbed within me? Put your hope in God, for I will yet praise him, my Savior and my God." We might suggest to our seniors who

are experiencing depression, discouragement, and grief that they use a hymnal to read or sing some of the wonderful old hymns and gospel songs of the church. Help seniors who are lonely and discouraged to think of the good things God has done. Remind them that when they are down, they should praise him. David remembered what God had done and offered hopeful praise.

3. *David knew that God was his stronghold, his strength, and the light at the end of the tunnel.* In Psalm 43:2a David said of God, "You are God my stronghold." Sometimes to gain victory over depression, we must help our seniors remember what God has done and is now doing. They will need to practice hope and praise. They will need to claim the victory of God who is our strength and victory.

4. *David knew there was light and truth to guide him, even though he might not see it at that moment.* Psalm 43:3 says, "Send forth your light and your truth, let them guide me; let them bring me to your holy mountain, to the place where you dwell." God's Word has power to help us each day. The Holy Spirit indwells believers with power. We may not see the end right now, but we must do as David did. David remembered what God had done. David practiced hope and praise. David claimed that God is strength.

We may not see the end right now, but we must do as David did. David remembered what God had done. David practiced hope and praise. David claimed God is strength.

5. *David went to the altar of God to find joy and delight.* Psalm 42:4-6a says, "These things I remember as I pour out my soul: how I used to go with the multitude, leading the procession to the house of God, with shouts of joy and thanksgiving among the festive throng. Why are you downcast, O my soul? Why so disturbed within me? Put your hope in God, for I will yet praise him, my Savior and my God."

When was the last time you invited your seniors to go with you to the altar? God desires that we place our lives on the altar.

I have done many military funerals. On my bookshelf at home, I have a shell given to me by a son after a military service for his dad. As I concluded the service, I watched the marines fold the flag with precision, care, and reverence. I heard the music and the twenty-one-gun salute. I felt a strong feeling of patriotism and pride in my country that I had not felt for a while. I had to be at a funeral to feel uplifted! I realized that it was the death of our Lord that brought about victory. Through the death and resurrection of Jesus, we have victory over depression.

There is a short poem that one of our members, Edith Kaufman, wrote in honor of her departed husband, Bud. I think it illustrates well the importance of both grieving and remembering.

It is sad to walk the road alone, instead of side by side;
But to all there comes a moment, when the ways of life divide.
You gave me years of happiness, then came sorrow and tears.
You left me beautiful memories I will remember through the years.

And finally, has life ever been summarized better than by Solomon in Ecclesiastes 3?

"There is a time for everything, and a season for every activity under heaven:

a time to be born and a time to die,
a time to plant and a time to uproot,
a time to kill and a time to heal,
a time to tear down and a time to build,
a time to weep and a time to laugh,
a time to mourn and a time to dance,
a time to scatter stones and a time to gather them,
a time to embrace and a time to refrain,
a time to search and a time to give up,
a time to keep and a time to throw away,
a time to tear and a time to mend,
a time to be silent and a time to speak,
a time to love and a time to hate,
a time for war and a time for peace.

"What does the worker gain from his toil? I have seen the burden God has laid on men. He has made everything beautiful in its time. He has also set eternity in the hearts of men; yet they cannot fathom what God has done from beginning to end. I know that there is nothing better for men than to be happy and do good while they live. That everyone may eat and drink, and find satisfaction in all his toil—this is the gift of God. I know that everything God does will endure forever; nothing can be added to it and nothing taken from it. God does it so that men will revere him" (Ecclesiastes 3:1-14).

As I close this chapter, as well as this book, my prayer is that each day we will find meaningful ways to strengthen the seniors God has entrusted to us and to fill their final years with memories that will last forever.

APPENDIX

62 Tips and Timesavers

1. Always take pictures of your senior adult activities. Hang them up on the church bulletin board. Have members of the group create clever captions for the pictures.
2. Subscribe to a popular magazine that will help keep you abreast of current senior adult trends, events, initiatives, legislation, and culture.
3. Set up a seniors' prayer chain.
4. Establish a telecare ministry.
5. Join a fellowship group of colleagues who work with senior adults in your area. If none exists, organize one. Meet periodically with these colleagues to share ideas and problems. This can be a great resource.
6. Do not meet in a room that is too big for your group. If your group is small, meet in a smaller room. This gives the feeling of being "full" or intimate. Always ensure your meeting place is casual and comfortable.
7. Avoid making promises you cannot keep.
8. Know when to ignore a disturbance during a meeting, and when not to! Someone with a hearing aid squealing or someone explaining something out loud to someone else may be overlooked. Someone with a health concern needs immediate attention.
9. If your group is small, combine with other senior groups for special events. Pool your resources. Share costs. Do not be afraid to invite another seniors' group to some of your activities, even if they are of another denomination.
10. Always deal with problems as they come up. Do not expect them to go away on their own. They will not. If someone is unhappy about something, deal with it privately and quickly.
11. Be involved in the community so you know what is going on locally.

12. Periodically keep track of your time for a week to see where it is really going.

13. Always arrive at the church or meeting place early enough to greet people as they arrive. Stay late for the same reason.

14. Develop programs that reflect the needs, interests, and energy levels of the people in your group. Normally older adults do not want long meetings.

15. Take two days away from the office to prepare for busy times during the year.

16. Develop realistic goals and expectations. Do not depend on immediate results to determine success or failure. The harvest is at the end of the age, not at the end of your meeting. Real results come later, often much later.

17. Take time to read several new books each year. Try to read a book on senior adult ministry, a book on time management, a book on theology, one of the "classics," and a couple of popular novels.

18. Do not be afraid to smile and laugh a lot. Senior adults love humor.

19. Let people be who they are. Watch your expectations.

20. Never cancel a meeting or event simply because not enough people showed up. You may need to adapt or change plans, but do not send everybody home. Let those who show up know that they are just as important as those who do not. Do not punish those who *do* come.

21. Keep up on current culture and trends in senior adult ministry. It's changing all the time.

22. Communicate availability. Do not give people the impression that you are too busy for them.

23. Have a hobby or some outside interest. Learn to play a musical instrument, start a collection of something, or take up a new sport.

24. Do not do everything yourself, even though you can do it better. Learn to delegate.

25. Do not neglect the shy or very quiet people in your group. Give them as much of your time and attention as possible.

26. Teach your leaders by your own example; be like players and coaches in ministry.

27. Even though most of the people you are working with have been married longer and have experienced more than you have, be a good role model.

28. Make sure every meeting and activity is well organized. This lets people know they are important and reduces problems.

29. Say what you mean in words that senior adults can understand. Avoid overly contemporary phrases that they may not understand.

30. Say something positive to each person. Compliment people often. *Please* and *thank you* are priceless words.

31. When talking with people, use personal illustrations to keep the message alive. Abstract ideas need concrete examples.

32. Do not take yourself or your circumstances too seriously. Nothing is ever as bad as you fear, and nothing is ever as good as you hope.

33. Be able to say, "I don't know." People will then listen better when you do know.

34. Avoid all double standards. Whatever goes for the leader should also go for you and your staff.

35. Deal with root causes, not symptoms, in your teaching. Rather than fighting or preaching, use discussion.

36. Attend some training event related to senior adults once a year. Never think you have learned it all.

37. Do not make threats. Be patient.

38. Do not worry about cliques. Instead, provide plenty of opportunities for everyone to interact with each other and to discover each other. Breaking up cliques is usually an exercise in futility and somewhat counterproductive.

39. When trying to improve the church, start with yourself.

40. Avoid counseling someone of the opposite sex in a private place. Keep the door open when you are counseling someone of the opposite sex.

41. Have a group to whom you can go for advice or counsel. You need the accountability and support that this will provide.

42. Never reveal a confidence that a person entrusts to you. No matter how well-intentioned it may be, doing so will almost always have disastrous results. There are exceptions, such as a life-threatening situation, but exceptions are rare.

43. Do not force yourself into lives where you might not be welcome.

44. Visit all of the local hospitals and hospices in your area. If possible, introduce yourself. Let them know who you are. Get acquainted.

45. Make learning the names of everyone a top priority. You will never have a ministry to them until you know and remember their names.

46. Avoid challenging or correcting people in front of the group. If someone offers an idea or thought that seems wrong, thank him or her for the contribution and continue asking for additional ideas.

47. It is best to handle problems privately on a one-to-one basis.

48. Keep a spare projector lamp handy for the next time you show a film or slides.

49. Learn the art of spontaneity. Call some people and invite them to go to breakfast with you the next day. Do something unpredictable now and then.

50. When leading a discussion, refrain from making overly positive or negative comments when people offer their opinions. Remain as neutral as possible. This will encourage openness and honesty.

51. Learn to say "no." Keep time for your family, your outside interests, and your personal growth.

52. Occasionally meet in the homes of church board members so they can see firsthand what the senior adult group is like.

53. Occasionally meet in the homes of various members; it involves them and they feel honored.

54. Become a listener. Learn to withhold your opinion on everything and just listen. You will be much more helpful that way.

55. Offer to help the chaplain at a local hospital or rest home with counseling or chapel services.

56. Do not be afraid to be a role model for your people. Whenever you can, take someone with you. Let people be witnesses to your life as you do the common, everyday things. Let them see you as a real person. Take someone with you when you visit in a home.

57. Prepare a good job description for yourself and for lay and/or professional staff.

58. Set up a mission project.

59. Prepare a senior adult newsletter, schedule meetings well in advance, and seek the group's input. Lack of communication can seriously "handicap" your ministry.

60. Develop good job descriptions for your volunteer leaders. Make sure they know exactly what is expected of them, as well as what is *not* expected of them. Provide them with good resources for the job that you have asked them to do.

61. Prepare a series of well thought out questions that you would use in a brainstorming session with your people to foster creativity. Allow ideas to flow without criticism. Evaluate only after the ideas have stopped.

62. Do not attempt to be someone you are not.

24 LIFESAVERS

1. Prepare a year's schedule of senior adult meetings, social events, and outreach events.

2. Keep a new members log including names, dates of membership, and other basic information for your own personal reference.

3. Keep a hymnal at your desk, and record at the top of the page each hymn and chorus that is used every Sunday. As you prepare the next Sunday's order of service, you will see if you are using certain songs too often or skipping others.

4. Prepare a counseling log in which you show who you met with, what you discussed, where you referred them to, and any progress.

5. Set up a long-range planning guide for the senior adult ministry.

6. Maintain a visitation log that contains every visit, date, purpose, and mileage. This is a good reference for your own personal use, but also serves as records for IRS and for your ministry reports. Highlight home visits, hospital visits, and denominational or community religious meetings with different-colored pens.

7. Always keep thorough records of all counseling sessions, recording the date, a brief synopsis of the session, and signed counseling forms.

8. Keep a ministry journal. Each week record and evaluate what you did with the group. Describe contacts with people, and reflect on each one. This will help you organize your thoughts and remember important events.

9. Always have at least one devotional, sermon, or talk "in the can" for emergency use. It will come in handy when your guest speaker does not show up or your musical group does not arrive.

10. Select several seasonal activities, and prepare and plan them in detail.

11. Have one notebook that has all church policies, constitution, and official board minutes (with actual motions highlighted). You may be surprised at how little the number of "official motions" or actual decisions are made.

12. Get a good refillable calendar that will enable you to plan your activities at least a year in advance. If you do not know where you are

going, you probably will not get there.

13. Prepare a resource file, filing system, or some other system that you personally will need in the future.

14. Keep a log of every meal you have in your home with church members and friends. Have a guest book to pass around the table after the meal, and take a picture of the dinner group. Put the pictures in a photo album with some simple notes of what you served and what your guests' interests and background are.

15. Keep a supply of games and social ideas handy. You never can tell when you will need them.

16. Set up a "Milestones and Setbacks" log, either on your computer or on hard copy.

17. Listen to the music that senior adults listen to. Radio programs and television will help you stay current. Be informed about senior happenings.

18. Keep a running list of potential new members, utilizing visitors, friends, and regular attenders who are not members.

19. Prepare a "referral file" for crisis counseling. If you feel inadequate or unsure of yourself, do not hesitate to refer people to professionals who have the appropriate training and experience.

20. Be involved in a small group.

21. Prepare a good service project. Get your group involved in at least one service project each year. Service projects not only give senior adults a chance to make a positive contribution to someone's life, but they also are great for building community.

22. Prepare a drama. This gives more senior adults a chance to use their talent and be in the limelight.

23. Have telephone numbers handy for lawyers, hospitals, funeral homes, churches, and hospice.

24. Have an excellent filing system for illustrations, sermons, ideas, and resources.

TOP WEB SITES FOR SENIOR ADULT ISSUES

Here are eight great Web sites for issues related to seniors. You may want to save these for future reference. This list is from Abstracts on Aging, the quarterly newsletter of John C. Lincoln Senior Apartments (Winter 2000).

- Access America for Seniors:
  http://www.seniors.gov
  Dedicated to 'providing government services electronically,' this site links to and organizes Federal government information that pertains to the concerns of senior adults.

- Administration on Aging:
  http://www.aoa.dhhs.gov
  Gateway site for the large amount of senior-related information on the Net.

- American Association of Retired Persons (AARP):
  http://www.aarp.org
  Provides in-depth information on a variety of senior-related concerns.

- Medical Rights Center:
  http://www.medicarerights.org/medicarerights/main
  The Medicare Rights Center (MRC) was established in 1989 by Whitney North Seymour, Jr. to provide free counseling services to Medicare beneficiaries who cannot afford private assistance. Since its founding, MRC has assisted more than 600,000 people with Medicare-related issues.

- National Senior Citizens Law Center:
  http://nsclc.org
  Focuses on legal issues that 'affect the security and welfare of older persons with limited income.'

- SeniorLaw Home Page:
  http://www.seniorlaw.com
  Information about Elder Law (Elderlaw), Medicare, Medicaid, estate planning, trusts and the rights of the elderly and disabled.

- Social Security Online:
  http://www.ssa.gov
  Official Web site of the Social Security Administration.

- Third Age:
  http://www.thirdage.com
  Billed as 'the Web for grown-ups,' this is an online magazine to help seniors enjoy the best years of their lives.

ENDNOTES

Introduction

1. From the video *Redefining Retirement* (Del Webb Corporation. Corporate Headquarters: 6001 N. 24th Street, Phoenix, Arizona 85016, 1-800-808-8080; 1994).

2. Win and Charles Arn, *Catch the Age Wave* (Grand Rapids, MI: Baker Books, 1993), 27-28.

3. Arnold S. Brown, *The Social Processes of Aging & Old Age* (Englewood Cliffs, NJ: Prentice-Hall, Inc., 1990), 16.

4. *Redefining Retirement* video, Del Webb Corporation.

5. Arn, *Catch the Age Wave*, 7-8.

Chapter 1

1. *Redefining Retirement* video

2. Win and Charles Arn, *Catch the Age Wave* (Grand Rapids, MI: Baker Books, 1993), 7.

3. Arn, *Catch the Age Wave*, 29.

4. *How Do I Find It? A Guide to Long/Short Term Care Options in the Northwest Valley* (Surprise, AZ: Northwest Valley Regional Community Council, 1998), 4-11.

5. Ibid. (Reprinted by permission.)

6. Ibid.

Chapter 2

1. J. Oswald Sanders, *Spiritual Leadership* (Chicago, IL: Moody Bible Institute of Chicago, 1967), 110.

2. Gary McIntosh and Glen Martin, *Finding Them, Keeping Them: Effective Strategies for Evangelism and Assimilation in the Local Church* (Nashville, TN: Broadman and Holman Publishers, 1992), 9.

3. George Barna, *The Power of Vision: How You Can Capture and Apply God's Vision for Your Ministry* (Ventura, CA: Regal Books, 1992), 28.

4. Charles L. Chaney and Ron S. Lewis, *Design for Church Growth* (Nashville, TN: Broadman Press, 1977), 18.

Chapter 3

1. In attempting to attribute this quote, I found it is similar in parts to quotes credited to both Helen Keller and Edward Everett Hale.

2. Neil T. Anderson, *Victory Over the Darkness: Realizing the Power of Your Identity in Christ* (Ventura, CA: Regal Books, 2000), 204.

3. Anderson, *Victory Over the Darkness*, 204.

Chapter 4

1. Abstracts on Aging, The Quarterly Newsletter of John C. Lincoln Senior Apartments (Winter, 2000), 2.

2. Win and Charles Arn, *The Master's Plan for Making Disciples* (Pasadena, CA: Church Growth Press, 1982), 104-105.

3. Michael Slater, *Stretcher Bearers: Giving and Receiving the Gift of Encouragement and Support* (Ventura, CA: Regal Books, 1985), 151.

Chapter 5

1. *The Golden Years: Riding the Crest*, Serendipity Support Group Series (Littleton, CO: Serendipity House, 1990), 28.

2. Doug Manning, *The Gift of Significance* (Hereford, TX: In-Sight Books, 1992), 5, 7.

3. Manning, *The Gift of Significance*, 8.

4. Edgar N. Jackson, *For the Living* (Des Moines, IA: The Meredith Publishing Company, 1963), 21.

5. Manning, *The Gift of Significance*, 31.

6. Manning, *The Gift of Significance*, 31.

7. Manning, *The Gift of Significance*, 32.

8. Manning, *The Gift of Significance*, 33.

9. Manning, *The Gift of Significance*, 35-38.

10. Manning, *The Gift of Significance*, 44.

11. Manning, *The Gift of Significance*, 46.

12. Manning, *The Gift of Significance*, 79.

13. Manning, *The Gift of Significance*, 80.

14. Gary Collins, *How to Be a People Helper: You Can Help the Others in Your Life* (Santa Ana, CA: Vision House Publishers, 1976), 13.

15. Collins, *How to Be a People Helper*, 33-54.

16. Collins, *How to Be a People Helper*, 46-47.

17. Ray Stedman, *Folk Psalms of Faith* (Glendale, CA: Regal Books, 1973), 201-218.

Simply
Strategic
volunteers
Empowering People
for Ministry
TONY MORGAN
TIM STEVENS